STICKING WITH IT

A SEA KAYAK ODYSSEY AROUND BRITAIN

Rowland Woollven

ROWLAND WOOLLVEN

Matador
9 Priory Business Park,
Wistow Road
Kibworth Beauchamp
Leicester LE8 0RX, UK
Tel: (+44) 116 279 2299
Fax: (+44) 116 279 2277
Email: books@troubador.co.uk
Web: www.troubador.co.uk/matador

ISBN 978-1783062-270

British Library Cataloguing in Publication Data.
A catalogue record for this book is available from the British Library.

Typeset in Aldine by Troubador Publishing Ltd, Leicester, UK
Printed and bound in the UK by TJ International, Padstow, Cornwall

Matador is an imprint of Troubador Publishing Ltd

*Doing what you want to do isn't a question of can you or
can't you, yes or no, but deciding what your ultimate desire
and capability is and then figuring out the steps to
accomplishment. It's "I'm going to. Now how?
What gear will I need?
What skills will I need?
What will it cost?
When will it happen?*

When I succeed, what next?"

Audrey Sutherland: Paddling North

Author's Note

Throughout this narrative, distances are measured in
nautical miles except where noted otherwise.
And 'stick' is the colloquial name for a Greenland
paddle, as used by the Inuit.

Contents

Maps in the Text

Colour Plates

(All pictures by Rowland Woollven unless otherwise credited.)

1. Cath and Rowland at the boat launch, April 2008. (N. Dennis)
2. Day 2: Across the Bristol Channel.
3. Off the entrance to the River Mersey.
4. Mirror seas. (C. Tanner)
5. In the Sound of Jura. (C. Tanner)
6. Looking to the Small Isles from Ardnamurchan.
7. West coast weather – Point of Stoer.
8. Return to Cape Wrath – probably not what the cardiologist had in mind! (C. Tanner)
9. One of the many storms that hit us in California.
10. What seemed like a perfect evening at Aldeburgh…
11. …and what faced us the following morning.
12. Waiting for the sea to return in Foulness Ranges. (B. Bramley)
13. Our second night run down the Essex coast.
14. The third corner – North Foreland in Kent.
15. Dungeness, after the storm.
16. A long landing in west Sussex.
17. Through the Bat Hole, east Dorset. (B. Bramley)
18. Furthest west in 2011 – the Bill of Portland. (B. Bramley)
19. Sky signs warning of the impending storms.
20. After the storm – the day we left Looe. (B. Bramley)
21. The aftermath of landing through seaweed at Fowey.

Illustrations in the text

(All pictures by Rowland Woollven unless otherwise credited.)

Prologue

The water was unbelievably cold. I could only gasp and try to hang on to the upturned kayak whilst wondering how to get back to the shore. At last the initial shock responses subsided a little and I made slow, and ever so painful, progress towards safety. If nothing else, this first and very short voyage in the kayak I had built myself had taught me an important lesson about dressing for immersion. Shorts, plimsolls, a T shirt and an old double chamber lifejacket were inadequate preparation for falling into icy cold water. Especially in a flooded gravel pit in North Kent in December. Crawling out of the water led to an only marginally less unpleasant state of being whipped by the cold wind off the Thames marshes, creating a fire of hot points all over my largely exposed skin. I was about 13 years old.

★

As a young boy in the 1950's and '60's, I was given an incredible amount of freedom by my parents to go wherever and do whatever I wanted in the countryside around our home. Often this meant long, all day rides on my single gear bike, exploring the marshes that lay alongside the Thames and getting into all sorts of unlikely adventures. My mother showed little concern; she was fairly sure that I would turn up when I got hungry, although I was often wet and usually muddy! The only restriction that I remember was laid down by my father, who insisted that if the adventures involved water, I had to be wearing a life jacket – swimmer or not. Some of my energy was channelled into the local Cub Scout pack, and as the pack fed into the local Sea Scout Troop as we got older, I inevitably became a Sea Scout, complete with naval uniform. This meant more activities on water, mainly on the Thames but also including a fine selection of gravel pits.

Where the impetus for kayaking came from, I cannot recall; most of our scouting activities were cutter and raft oriented, but there must have been a kayak in there somewhere. A little later I started into the process of joining the Army, eventually following my father into the Royal Engineers and it was whilst away at school at the very beginning of that track that I built my very first kayak.

Activities in my early military life included compulsory 'adventure training', although in my case I never felt compelled and was perfectly happy to go walking, climbing or canoeing wherever I was sent. As a young officer I was encouraged to gain qualifications in various outdoor activities so that I could take soldiers out into the hills and onto the water, and this led to my first 'tickets' as a mountain leader, climbing instructor and canoeing instructor. I was also fortunate to spend the first five years of my career as a commando engineer officer in 45 Commando Group, a 1500-strong commando force based in Scotland and concentrating on operating in the mountains and Arctic.

Over the following decades I spent time in different parts of the world, but was always able to spend time on the hills and on the water (both for business and pleasure!) I also met and married Carol, who subsequently displayed considerable patience as I added voluntary separation on expeditions to that imposed by the demands of Army life. She also put up with the slowly increasing collection of kayaks that became part of our garden decorations.

I was always able to get away to attend civilian kayaking events and meetings, especially so when I found myself commanding the Joint Service Mountain Training Centre (which also, rather confusingly, covered kayaking in all its disciplines). It was during this period that I attended one of the annual sea kayaking symposiums held on Anglesey and attracting world-leading paddlers from many countries.

To put it mildly the noise was deafening, so much so that Chris Duff, paddler extraordinaire with circumnavigations of Britain, Iceland, Ireland and South Island, New Zealand to his credit, had upped sticks and moved to a tent upwind and 100 metres away. He was still being kept awake! The rest of us played on, oblivious to everything but creating a beat to accompany whatever CD was blaring out from the corner. We were in the front room of Nigel Dennis – founder of Sea Kayaking UK and with Paul Caffyn one of the two people to have first circumnavigated mainland Great Britain by sea kayak – at the 'end of week' party after the May Anglesey Sea Kayak Symposium and the following courses week. All the surviving coaches, trip leaders and helpers were there, unwinding with a vengeance. In one corner sat the coaching director of the British Canoe Union, saucepan on his head and keeping time with the music by hammering on it with a wooden spoon!

Looking around the room, through something of a deafening haze, I realised that of the 17 or so people who had paddled around the British Isles at that time, no fewer than half were here. And so, in that moment, the idea was born. One day I was going to join that club.

Genesis

Fast forward a few years to another May symposium and to a 5 Star training course group gathered in another room in the same building. To break the ice with this group, who were understandably apprehensive about what Fiona Whitehead and I were about to do with them over the next three days, we were talking about what we had all done, and the paddling plans we had for the future. Fiona had the previous year become the first woman to paddle around the 'greater' British Isles – Britain and Ireland – and had a deserved reputation as a committed and skilful paddler and coach. When it came to my turn to speak, I described some of my expeditions to Alaska and western British Columbia, and then said that the year after I left the Army, my plan was to paddle around Britain. I recall saying 'I don't mind whether I do it solo or accompanied, supported or self-contained, or some mix of all that, I just want to see the coastline of my country.'

Towards the end of the week, Cath Tanner, one of the students and an outdoor instructor and lecturer at a college in Cornwall, approached me and said that she would be interested in doing the trip, if I was looking for someone to paddle with. And that, quite simply, is how the team came together and the whole project crossed the start line. We settled on 2008 for the trip as I was going to leave the Army in the summer of 2007, after 35 years. That timeframe would also give Cath the opportunity to try and get a sabbatical from her lecturing post. She was, she told me, quite prepared to resign and come anyway if the college turned out to be unsympathetic towards the idea.

In early 2007, Cath and I met at the Outdoor Show in Birmingham to have a detailed talk about the plan and to sort out who was doing what in terms of getting kit and equipment ready for the trip. By the end, we had agreed proposals to put to various manufacturers and suppliers, hopefully to cut down the cost of what was likely to be a very expensive trip for us to undertake. We also divided the tasks of getting such things as maps and charts prepared and had started to think about where we could pre-position some items around the coast with friends we would pass.

Another thing we talked about was health and fitness. My particular concern was that I have a condition known as paroxysmal atrial fibrillation (AF). This is a heart condition where the top chambers of the heart go out of sync with the lower chambers and as a result, you lose effective circulation. If the condition is allowed to persist, bad things can happen… I had suffered from this before and was on medication which generally controlled it. Known triggers for the condition include emotional and physical stress, dehydration and a lack of sleep; standard parts of the majority of major expeditions. I had been cleared to try the circumnavigation by both the cardiologist and GP who looked after me, but I needed Cath to understand the problem, the possible implications, and the actions that might be required. She did, and was very supportive throughout our adventure.

By this stage, Carol and I had bought a house on the coast

near Oban in west Scotland, so another decision had to be made as to where and when Cath and I were going to start the following year. Cath lived in Plymouth, so there and Oban were the two obvious choices, but both had significant drawbacks. We expected to take about six months to complete the trip, and mid-April to mid-September traditionally offered the most favourable weather window for a circumnavigation. Starting in Plymouth or Oban in mid-April would put us either on the tip of the south west peninsula or on the far north west and north coasts at a time when there was still a better than average chance of poor weather. We saw the crux as being the far north west and north coasts (although Cornwall and north Devon held their own share of demons in our collective paddling memories), so a start point somewhere on the west coast allowing us to warm into the trip and get to the north at the start of summer seemed the best bet. Then we decided that it would be nice to pass through the Anglesey symposium whilst it was on, so we started to look for somewhere in north Devon or south Wales, from which it would take about three weeks to get to Anglesey. And so the start point became Ilfracombe in north Devon. This would give us, we hoped, a sheltered harbour start and finish to the trip, avoid the need for a big surf start and finish. It did have the drawback of making us do a major crossing of the Bristol Channel very early on. We planned to get around this by going east to Porlock and making a 12 mile crossing from there, something well within our comfort zone. Having determined the start point, deciding on the day of departure was just a question of going back two and a half weeks from the date of the symposium – and so it became 14 April 2008.

PART ONE
A Broken Dream

Preparations

Now that we had a plan, we started in earnest to get things together. The boats and suitable clothing were our main concerns because of their cost. For many years I had been one of Nigel Dennis's sponsored paddlers, so for me the boat was not actually a problem. For Cath, however, it was a major consideration. Fortunately Nigel decided that he would give Cath a boat for the trip on the proviso that she passed her 5 Star assessment, for the top personal performance award, first. We settled on an Explorer High Volume for me and an Explorer Low Volume for Cath. This meant that whilst we retained the same hull shape and hence basic speed, the boats were individually fitted to our rather different body sizes (I am over a foot taller than Cath, and rather heavier). Just as we were getting them, Nigel decided to change the logo for his company to a Celtic dragon and a hundred of a small sticker version of this found their way all over the upper deck of my boat leading to the name Dragonquest. Cath's choice of boat colour was a rather vibrant pink and so the boat was naturally decorated with feathers and became 'Tickled Pink'!

Another friend, Dave Felton, ran a specialist kayak retail operation called Knoydart. With his help and introduction, we approached a US firm called Kokatat. These are the makers of specialist sea kayak clothing and I had used their separate paddle jackets and overtrousers for many years and was very pleased with their performance. To our surprise, Kokatat readily agreed to sponsor us and gave us each a touring jacket and pair of overtrousers together with a MSfit buoyancy aid. These were really comfortable, and had enough pockets to satisfy even the most enthusiastic carrier of 'bits and bobs'. Kokatat also gave us a touring spraydeck each, but these were less successful as the fit on the Explorer cockpit rims was not ideal for either of us, and the positioning of the body tube did not seem quite right either.

As a result we approached Seals Skirts, another US firm making high class spraydecks and they supplied us with a 'Seals Shocker' spraydeck each. Mine performed superbly, was totally waterproof and three years after the expedition it was still going strong. Cath had a minor problem in that her rather shorter body length led to the buoyancy aid rubbing on the front of the deck. This created a wear patch which was addressed by the application of seam sealant at regular intervals throughout the trip. Again, Cath's deck was still going strong years later.

I usually paddle using a Greenland style paddle as used by the Inuit and often referred to as 'a stick'. A friend from Denmark, Martin Nissen, not only built me two paddles for the trip, but also caught a ferry across the North Sea then drove to me to hand-deliver them as well. Cath used her usual Werner paddle, and was totally happy with it (although we had the regular wrestling match getting the two halves apart every few days). We each carried split versions of our paddles as a back-up, but neither of us had to resort to using them.

I already had much of the chart coverage of the coastline; the areas I did not have created a large bill, but that was unavoidable. Cath managed to persuade her employers (Duchy College, Cornwall) to support her with a set of charts and also with map coverage of the entire coast. This turned out to be a not insignificant pile of paper! By this time also, Cath had gained agreement for a six month sabbatical from the college, so her job was safe for her to return to, although she would not be paid during her absence.

Knoydart were very supportive and gave us generous discounts on everything we bought from them, mainly the hardware of flares and other paddling-specific goodies. Local shops in Plymouth and Oban provided a lot of help and went out of their way to get items in for us. Lastly, and by no means least, Pole Position, the internet company that looks after my website, agreed to add a map page to the site and then put 'pins' in it as we made our way around the coast so that people could follow our progress (or lack of it) on the web. We decided not to have a daily blog or diary because we both felt that we would then be in danger of somehow being held accountable by others. We felt that having just the map meant that we could retain 'our' control over 'our' expedition. For much the same reasons, we decided initially not to formally be 'in aid' of anything or anyone when we started the trip. Interestingly, many people we met could not quite understand this, and could not accept that we were doing the trip just because we wanted to. In the end, we just told everyone that we were raising money for the RNLI, and this became 'official' by about mid-way when we got hold of some stickers and decorated the sides of the boats with them. One of the problems this created was people spontaneously giving us donations. These we then looked after until we could get to a collecting box or RNLI station where we handed it over. I became a lot more pro-active after the trip and after every presentation I gave, I actively asked and encouraged people to donate.

We knew that a major problem would be keeping in touch with home. Much of the coastline is, in mobile phone terms, remote and despite carrying a variety of phone SIM cards we knew there would be places where we could not communicate. Particularly in the north west, we did indeed spend a lot of time in the evenings roaming the local areas looking for an elusive signal. Marine radio (VHF) coverage is also not guaranteed, so there were genuine concerns over what we could do if we needed help in a real emergency. Jen Kleck, a friend of mine in San Diego and owner of an operation called Aqua-Adventures, came to our rescue by giving me a SPoT messenger unit. This device works in conjunction with GPS satellites to provide nearly world-wide rescue coverage at a fraction of the cost of an EPIRB or satellite phone. A choice of buttons meant that you could let a pre-planned list of people know where you were, or let a primary contact know that you needed help short of a rescue, or you could press the '911' button. This last button would initiate a full-scale search and rescue operation. It was the daily 'we're here' button that we used; and it was this that kept us in touch with Lucy at Pole Position, enabling her to move the pins around our map.

We decided to carry about five days of food in each kayak, and cook together. This meant we would be looking for a shop about once a week, although as we got into more remote areas we knew we would be likely to be carrying more, and shopping less frequently. Fortunately our tastes were not that different and for most of the trip we cooked main meals for two, although breakfasts were always separate. Cath does not like porridge and I do not like noodles! Lunch systems went through many changes – buns, bagels, pies and malt loaves being just a few of the variations. On occasion we bought fish and chips or other ready or pub meals wherever we landed and, more rarely, we bought a proper restaurant meal. We found that this was a rather expensive way of catering, so we did not indulge too often. Over the course of the five months we were on the expedition, we both changed shape dramatically; I lost weight I could afford, and Cath lost weight she could not!

Getting the boats to and from the water each day is one of the major trials of this sort of expedition, so Cath opted to buy a German-made trolley which broke down into stowable sections, although the pneumatic wheels always had to remain on Cath's back deck. It worked really well over all sorts of terrain, but did manage to have a puncture whilst we were at Aberdovey, necessitating a trip to both a chandlers and a garage to sort out the problem.

So, in two houses, the piles of gear were getting larger as the day of departure got closer. A few days before we were due to start, Carol and I drove south to Tavistock to stay with my brother and father; from there it would be about a two hour drive to Ilfracombe on Monday 14 April 2008.

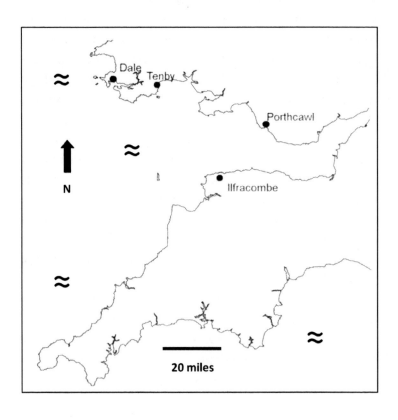

Map 1 – Early Days: Ilfracombe to Dale

Early Days

Packing at Ilfracombe was the usual nightmare. Both of us had brought too much kit, and the well intended assistance of friends and family actually made things more difficult. Eventually at about midday we got away, heading straight into an adverse tide and wind. This did not matter too much as both of us were suffering from the effects of emotional farewells. Although Carol and I were used to being separated (our first year of being married saw me being away for 10 months) it is never easy or pleasant to say goodbye, but at least during this period of absence there was little fear of being shot at! Getting used to our very heavy boats, Cath and I plodded east through some rather bumpy seas, not at all the gentle start we had imagined, until the tide told us we were going no further. A large tide race and overfall formed off the east side of Heddon Mouth meant we had to end the day and a very bumpy landing over large cobbles brought us to the feet of some holiday makers, who seemed rather surprised at our being out so early in the season. We decided to forego the delights of carrying everything up to the nearest patch of grass (it was rather a long way away) and settled for the first of many nights on cobbled beaches.

Much to our surprise, we awoke to a flat calm sea with no wind. Because of this, the plan of continuing east to

Packing at Ilfracombe (C. Woollven)

Porlock and crossing from there was rapidly abandoned in favour of the more direct 18 mile crossing to Wales. This proved straightforward, if somewhat stressful because of the shipping traffic into Swansea and Bristol, until three miles from the end when the wind got up against the by now outgoing tide. That last hour was a bit of a struggle past Nash Bank and we eventually landed just after high water at Nash Cwm. We were somewhat tired, but very pleased to have got one of the major crossings of the whole trip out of the way on only the second day. The flush of success led us to think about getting across Swansea Bay to the Mumbles the next day, but that was not to be. After a very chilly night, we faced the first of many long portages to the sea which was just under half a mile away. Some parts of the country have a large tidal range – the difference in height between low and high tide – and when this combines with a gently sloping sea floor, the sea can go out a very long way indeed. Classical examples in the UK include Morecambe Bay (scene of many tragedies over the years), the Wash (where King John lost his treasure!) and the Bristol Channel. At moments like these, the trolley came into its own, but we still had to walk back and forth four times each, and all this took a lot of time and effort. Our troubles were not over when we finally launched. There was an evil little cross-current running off the ledge and in avoiding being swept into the undercut rocks to my right, I totally mistimed the exit and ended up soaked. Cath had an even worse time of it, getting caught in the undercut and having to bail out of her boat. On her second attempt, she came out at high speed with her legs still not in the cockpit, and her boat fully flooded! It was a very wet pair of paddlers who set off in a strong cold wind down the coast towards Ogmore. The Force 6 easterly did its best to push us offshore, so we hugged the coast, getting caught in amongst lots of small reefs as we did so. Off Ogmore the wind got up even more, so we decided enough was enough and we landed at the end of the beach. Because it was still near low water, we had a very long trolley over the sand to get to the nearest slip, next to which we promptly camped. This evoked some muttering from passers-by, but any sympathy we felt for them by disturbing their walk was offset by our distaste at the amount of dog poo that had to be removed to make spaces for the tents. Later in the day, near the top of the tide, the local stand-up long boarders came out to play, and they were universally supportive of what we were up to. It was the first time either of us had seen these in action, and it was fascinating to watch them catch some really long rides on the waves.

After another cold night (which was getting to be something of a theme), we set off under another Force 6. We did not think we would get across to the Mumbles, but we also recognised that our campsite was 'sub-optimal', so we had to go on if at all possible. We passed Porthcawl at a rapid rate, but then hit yet more reefs and rough water heading down towards Sker Point. By now the wind was rising again, so we pulled in after the point and sought shelter in the dunes at the top of the beach. The forecast was not good; another major low pressure system was inbound, bringing with it gale force easterlies, so it seemed we might be here for a couple of days as it blew through. And that was how it turned out; two days sheltering from bitterly cold gale force easterly winds. The one good thing about being beached was that Carol came and found us, bringing with her some items that we had not included at Ilfracombe, but now thought we needed, and taking away some things which we realised were not needed at this stage of the trip. The down side to that was that I had a second farewell in a week, and that was something I could well have done without.

Two days later, the sea was flat, and the wind had dropped, so we crossed to the Mumbles, speaking to and being waved at by the Coastguard as we passed. Another major crossing was done and we only had Carmarthen Bay to go before we could relax a bit, or so we thought. We carried on along the coast to Port Eynon where landing was straightforward, but finding a place to camp was rather more awkward. Eventually we just ignored the plethora of 'no camping' signs and set up next to the lifeboat station (that was to become another theme for the trip). We had a pleasant evening during which I found a lady who was prepared to give us water, and also allow us to recharge both the phones and the VHF. In return, and over a cup of tea, I listened to tales of a youth spent in the Amazon Basin, yet again proving that there are lots of adventurous people out there who do not feel the need to broadcast their every movement. Just as we were going to bed, we were visited by an off-duty Coastguard member. She was the operator I had been talking to earlier in the day and we found out that the Coastguard were 'in dispute with management'. As a result, we would only get emergency search and rescue cover each time they went on strike. This went on for nearly the whole of our trip, and eventually we gave up trying to log our passage plans with them, relying on being able to call for help if something went wrong (which inevitably it did). Although the evening had been fine, we awoke to a bad forecast of a Force 6 rising Force 7 easterly and torrential rain. As the next leg included the last of the major crossings in this section, Carmarthen Bay, we decided to give it a day and see what the weather was like on the morrow. And so we had a quiet day. The rain eased later on and we spent some time in the only café open at that stage of the season. A cliff walk resulted in us at last getting a signal for the phones, and then it was back to bed after a long chat with the coxswain of the lifeboat.

The following day started out very pleasantly, with a superb sunshine paddle down to Worm's Head. Here the height of the tide allowed us to cut inside to Burry Holms, where we repeated the manoeuvre and scraped over a sand bank into the eastern edge of Carmarthen Bay. Crossing this proved somewhat trying. In the bay are two bombing ranges, and around the inside edge are small arms and experimental explosive ranges. All of them were in use, so we had to set a GPS track going from point to point avoiding all the range danger areas. The alternative would have been a 19 mile direct crossing across the mouth of the bay, but this would put us a long way out in the middle if the weather deteriorated as was forecast. Setting off, the weather was fine, but within half an hour, we were enveloped in thick mist, giving us no visibility at all. This did not really matter as we were constrained to follow our

GPS track, but it would have been nice to at least see both the coastline and any inbound aircraft. Paddling in these conditions is akin to skiing in a whiteout – or trying to do anything with a grey bin bag over one's head. My eyes sought constantly for anything solid to look at. Marker buoys and the occasional sea bird were a poor substitute for being able to see the shoreline. As it was, we could only paddle the course, wincing each time something overflew us and then dropped its bombs away to our left. Crossing the flats in the middle of the bay, the sea state got up, as did the wind; we could not change our direction to cope with either more easily, so a very unpleasant three hours followed. I was getting very occasional glimpses of the dunes at the back of the bay, but Cath, whose eyesight is not as sharp as mine, saw nothing other than me and the occasional marker buoy for the whole crossing. She definitely did not appreciate the experience – 'the only thing I've seen for the last three hours is the back of your boat and the bloody sea'. Eventually we came within sight of the western shore, but our pleasure at seeing land again was offset by seeing the size of the surf we would have to land through. So we carried on to Tenby, landing eventually through small surf in the sheltered corner of the bay. We were a very relieved, and frazzled, pair of paddlers! We carried everything up onto the concrete sea defences, and set up camp looking across to the bright lights of Tenby (the temptations of which we managed to avoid). The highlight of the late afternoon was a raid by an exceptionally cheeky gull which carried off a malt loaf, pursued at high speed by an affronted Cath. She recovered the loaf, but it did have some rather large spear-shaped indentations in it. We still ate it.

St George's Day, 23 April, started well. We got up to a quiet sea with some swell running off the points. Our plan was to have a short (-ish) day, going only as far as Stackpole Quay or Broadham. We were both a bit tired after crossing Carmarthen Bay, and the very last thing we wanted was another long, tiring paddle… We got to Stackpole relatively early, but the land around there is all National Trust, so the possibilities for camping were not that good. This was neither the first nor last time that made me long for Scotland and its far more sensible access laws. Our reception here when asking about the possibility of camping also started to confirm our feelings that people rarely sat on the fence in their views. We were either welcomed with open arms and helped to an embarrassing extent, or we were cold-shouldered or even met with hostility. There seemed to be no middle ground in people's attitude. In the harbour lay the range safety boat for Castlemartin Ranges, our next potentially serious section of coast. Cath and I had previously paddled this (in rather lumpy conditions) and knew that escape routes were notable only by their absence. Speaking to the range boat crew revealed a serious dilemma. The weather forecast they had would leave us beached for several days and also leave a residual swell and wild conditions along this part of the coast. Their recommendation was 'go today – or wait a week'. Neither of us particularly fancied a committing paddle at the end of the day, but the camping situation was 'adverse', so we did not have any realistic alternative. The range was still operating until late afternoon with main battle tanks on pre-Iraq firing practice so we could not start along the range wall until after 4 p.m. Just for once it was me being made to wait for a range to close rather than being one of those firing and causing others to wait. An aquatic case of 'gamekeeper turned poacher'! So we waited, then hopped around to the last beach, and then met the range boat off Meadsfoot Point.

Once we had clearance, we set off. By now, of course, the tide was against us, and a big Atlantic swell was running in across the stream. Swell can be a frightening component of what mariners call 'sea state'. This is the term used to describe the resultant appearance of water flowing into things, bouncing off things, being constricted by underwater obstacles to its progress, being squeezed between gaps, having wind generated swell from far off storms running into shore, and of course the wind itself. All of these factors can combine to create mountains of jumbled water, breaking heavily and unpredictably. In our case, the swell pushed up the current into violent, heaving stacks of water – committing, if not downright dangerous, paddling conditions. St Govan's Head, the start of the most serious section, was horrible. In extremely advanced conditions, we were making only 0.8 knots – clawing our way around it, going in as close as we dared. The range boat crew decided to escort us very closely. They were so close that Cath, who was having an unpleasant time of it, invited them to 'go away' (or words to that effect). They were too close and seriously distracting her. Eventually, having rounded the Head and at last going a little more quickly (if not any more easily), the range boat left us, having informed me that they had let the Coastguard know where we were and what we were doing. This rather implied that they thought we were going to need rescuing, which was not a comforting thought in the circumstances. Anyway, for the next two hours we fought our way to the end of the range and around Linney Head. Here we encountered the biggest seas I had ever paddled in – and bigger than I ever want to paddle in again. Mountains of water grew and collapsed in unpredictable forms as we looked at them in alarm. This was way outside any of our experience, and watching a trawler twist and turn, bobbing like a cork in the white water as it fought to get through the race was truly frightening. At times it completely disappeared from view, which was disconcerting given our relative sizes. Whilst considering the option of an 'inside line' between some islets and the cliff, a huge swell set came through and the whole area exploded into a maelstrom of hideous white water. That forced us to go the outside route, making us surf 20 to 30 foot waves, with absolutely no realistic chance of recovery or rescue if something went wrong. For the next 15 minutes, we paddled for our lives.

Breaking clear of the tide, still afloat, we took stock. Both of us were mentally and physically exhausted. The previous day had taken its toll, and the paddle we had just survived had badly shaken us. Neither of us could speak easily as our throats were raw from the effort of surviving. Neither of us had been able to take a drink for the last two hours, but both of us were now instantly desperate for a pee; the relief at being still alive was flooding our system in more ways than one! By now evening was drawing in, but from well over a mile out we could hear the surf running in to Freshwater West beach so landing there was out of the question. This committed us to paddling to Milford Haven, going inside the entrance and landing at West Angle beach, so we paddled on for another hour and a half, eventually landing at dusk. We were met on the beach by two of Cath's friends. They had been in intermittent contact throughout the day, and had bought us a fish supper in anticipation of our landing at Freshwater West. As a consequence of our having to paddle longer, it was now stone cold but nonetheless it was eagerly wolfed down. Their help carrying the boats up the beach to a small patch of grass next to the public toilets was very welcome, as was help in getting the tents up. Sadly, their efforts were poorly repaid, as we were both shocking company. We were by now reduced to monosyllabic replies as we were so tired. We thought we were in for a hard time when the local National Park warden turned up – I was fully expecting the 'you can't camp here' scenario. To our pleasant surprise, he took the line that 'you shouldn't really be camping here, but given what you're doing, it won't be a problem'. That was very welcome, and so to bed! Traditionally outdoor education theorists talk about the 'comfort zone' where we operate in safety and in comfort, without stress or fear. At the edge of the zone lies the 'breakdown zone' where things are likely to go calamitously wrong and be extremely stressful. Going beyond that, usually unwillingly, leads into the 'disaster zone' where real physical and psychological damage can be done. In paddling terms this had been the biggest day I had ever had, and Cath had found reserves she never knew she had. We had both been far outside of any 'comfort zone'.

The next day revealed bright sunshine but a Force 6-7 easterly wind howling over our heads. Moving was out of the question as we were both shattered from two hard days in succession. Cath's hands were spectacularly covered in blisters as she had been gripping her paddle rather hard for a long time the previous afternoon. So we had an admin day, washing kit and spreading everything out to dry in the sunshine. It also gave us a chance to catch up with all the small mending jobs that otherwise just did not get done. We walked into the village only to discover that the shelves in the store were distinctly bare as they were awaiting the delivery van! Nevertheless, we bought some bits and pieces and then rounded the day off with a café lunch and pub dinner. We had lots of visitors at our camp. Everyone was very supportive of the trip, even if we were declared insane on more than one occasion.

A pleasant start gave way to mist, then fog, then complete loss of visibility. The advantage of having this weather was that tankers are not allowed to enter or leave Milford Haven if there is less than one mile visibility, so at least we were not going to meet anything big in the fog as we crossed the channel. On the down side, we could not see a thing, so we relied on dead reckoning, backed up by the GPS. The crossing was relatively straightforward; the scary part was being able to hear small craft moving around, but having no idea of where the sound was coming from. We met a pilot boat at one of the cardinal mark buoys and then sprinted to the far side of the channel, turning to seaward and, we hoped, getting out of the Haven. However when we got near the exit point, the seas were large after two days of gales and very chaotic. It was not a particularly hard decision to abort. We decided not to cross back to West Angle, but to stay on the west side and go into Dale. Arriving here in thick mist was eerie; no-one was about and we got the firm impression of an apparently deserted village. There was a complete lack of anywhere to camp other than a small patch of grass right outside the village hall and we thought we would be pushing our luck to stay there. As it happened, that evening the hall was the venue for an annual live band performance; we would have got no sleep at all being camped there! A lady called Jane, who ran the local sailing school, came to our rescue, offering us a patch of gravel at the back of the boat shed to camp on. Very gratefully we set up the tents and hid from the rain. Moving between the tents was something of an obstacle course, what with all the boats, frames and paraphernalia spread around. Jane offered us full use of the school, so showers, teas and coffees were readily accepted. We walked around the village in the afternoon only to discover that Dale was indeed, to all intents and purposes, shut. At least the forecast was improving, so we hoped to be able to get away in the morning. We had already lost enough days to make reaching Anglesey in time for the symposium a doubtful prospect. Sleep that night was somewhat disturbed by the band, but the dancers finally broke up and went home at about 2 a.m.

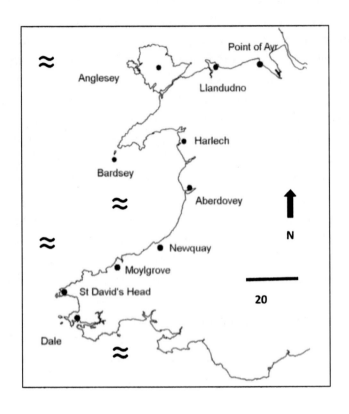

Map 2 – West Wales

West Wales

Leaving Dale – Part Two. It was something of a groundhog day today. The Haven was still and calm, and the forecast was favourable, so we packed up, said our farewells and left. When we got near to St Ann's Head, the large lumps of water were still there, with the occasional really large aggressive breaker coming through. Worse still, we could not make out the end of the disturbed zone, so if we entered it, we had no idea of what lay beyond our limited horizon. So we turned back into Dale, said 'hello' again, and repitched camp. Somewhat cross, we decided to walk up to the Head to get a better idea of what lay around the corner. From here we could at last see the extent of the zone of rough water and watch the size of some of the swells coming through and it was just as well we had not committed ourselves to going on earlier in the morning. We went back to the sailing school for lunch. In the afternoon we caught the bus into Milford Haven for a look around, which did not take long as all the cafés were shut, and a resupply run in Tesco. Even their café was shut! The weather and the forecast both looked good, so hopefully we would get out of the Haven in the morning.

We did. Although there were still respectable sized seas at St Ann's Head, we could at least this time see where the zone ended, so we went. The coast along to Jack Sound was very scenic, and it was a happy pair of paddlers that pulled in to the

West Wales - Ramsey Sound. (C. Tanner)

little harbour where the tourist boats set off from for the island sanctuaries of Skokholm and Skomer. We could see right across St Bride's Bay to Ramsey Sound, so we set off on what promised to be an uneventful crossing. About 20 minutes later, a thick blanket of fog rolled in from seaward, so we were once again in a quiet white circle about 100 metres across. The crossing was made scary by encountering a large tanker picking up a mooring to wait for clear weather to go round into Milford Haven, and bearable by seeing porpoise and puffins. The fog lasted right until we came to the rocks at the entrance to Ramsey Sound, where, thankfully, it lifted and we found ourselves pleasantly bathed in sunshine. Given that we were finally moving again, and that we had the tide in our favour for once, we decided not to go into Whitesands Bay, where both of us had scary memories of rather large surf landings in the past, but to push on round St David's Head and up to Abereiddi. Landing through surf can either be terrifying or great fun, depending on both your mood and that of the sea. Breakers can either 'spill', losing their power gradually or 'dump' where they dissipate power explosively. Sea kayakers tend to prefer spilling waves, but when big even these can be challenging verging on frightening. A sea kayak, especially one laden for an expedition, can be an unwieldy thing at the best of times and can prove difficult to control in surf. As a result surf landings were something we coped with when we were forced into them, rather than experiences we actively sought out. The seas off St David's Head were sufficiently big to make us think that the Welsh saints had it in for us, what with epics at St Govan's, St Ann's and now St David's Heads! We pushed through an awkward section of overfalls – disturbance created where the tidal stream runs over an underwater obstruction such as a reef or shelf – at the end of the Head and then ran close in up the coast to Abereiddi. Landing here through the surf had the potential to be trying, but responded to a bit of careful timing and energetic sprinting to get ashore safely. We camped at the edge of the beach car park and got some hotdogs from the van that was keeping the local surfers fed and watered. Seeing our increasingly frustrated attempts to make phone contact, one of the surfers offered us the use of his phone, so we were able to make two quick calls to let everyone know we were OK after yet another long day. The village seemed completely empty so we retired early. We were tired but rather pleased after a good day's paddle where we had covered another 24 miles of the journey.

What a night! A major storm hit us with big winds and lashing rain, together with something that sounded like material being ripped but once I determined it wasn't my tent I thought no more of it. The rain stopped early in the morning but the scene around the tents was one of carnage. As well as the expected large puddles, much of Cath's kit had been dragged out from the porch of her tent. We found a beach shoe about 30 metres away and both our deck bags had been attacked, mine to the extent that it was ripped apart. What had done all this remained a mystery… After an early breakfast, we were packing the boats when a car parked quite close to us and a man approached. My first thought was 'here we go again – you know you can't camp here' etc, but actually the conversation started 'Hi, my name's Spike – would you like to come for breakfast?'! It turned out that Spike was a paddler himself, but we never found out how he had found us. Having just had breakfast, his offer was reluctantly declined (that would not have happened later in the trip), but in the conversation as we packed we learned that a cat lived wild in the village, feeding itself by ripping open bin bags and scavenging the contents. It seemed likely that the 'wild cat of Abereiddi' had been the mystery source of destruction and chaos with our kit. We eventually got off, heading towards Strumble Head. All went well until just before the Head when the sea state rose and became rather challenging. The inside line between some rocky islets and the cliffs themselves looked horrible, but marginally better than the outside line running through large wave sets at a fast speed, so in we went and spent a sporting half hour threading our way through gaps and reefs. It was with considerable relief that we got ashore just under the footbridge to the lighthouse and had lunch in a very cold wind. We decided that Strumble Head was a mis-spelling, and should in fact be St Rumble's Head – that would be in keeping with the mauling we had received at the hands of the other Welsh saints' heads! Afterwards we passed Fishguard and paddled round into the estuary near Newport, where we camped in the dunes at the back of the beach, thawing out after a very cold day.

After a long trolley to the water's edge, we started the following day in the face of an unpromising forecast of NE Force 5, straight into our faces. And so it turned out. We clawed around every headland and across every bay for five miles before accepting that what we were doing was not terribly productive. We turned into Moelgrove, setting up camp at the top of the beach and then hid from the rain for the rest of the day. A motorist gave me a lift to the top of the cliffs to get a VHF signal to talk to the CG. Unfortunately my thermals by this stage were becoming a little ripe, so the windows on the vehicle were ostentatiously lowered to allow the smell out. I apologised profusely. In the afternoon we were visited by a couple walking two wolfhounds, so I had my dog fix; our own dog was a wolfhound and I always found I missed her whenever I was away from home. On an altogether different subject, we had passed some seals early in the morning, and it did cross my mind that their wonderfully spotted and ringed skins would make a really nice covering for a skin-on-frame kayak!

We stayed there the next day too. A Force 8 gale blew over us, with lots of heavy rain. Cath had inadvertently camped in the outflow of a stream, so we spent some time diverting the flow away from her tent. A walk up to a nearby garden centre café proved about a Grade 6 mountaineering route in crocs and beach shoes and both of us had major slips and slides. Our pre-lunch nap was disturbed by a voice asking if we were at home; this resulted in being taken by car back to a chalet for showers and a battery recharge, followed by a shopping run – thank you Mike. The rain stopped just after dinner, so we sorted ourselves out again; the forecast was favourable and the sea state had dropped right down. It seemed that all was looking good for the next day. That turned out to be the case. The seas off the first headland were a bit lumpy, but then the stream turned in our direction and with both that and the wind behind us, we fair flew along. Lunch was taken at Aberporth and tea at Newquay but not in quite such pleasant surroundings as there was raw sewage running across the beach and into the sea... I thought the approach was a little 'murky'… Looking for a better pitch, we went on to Aberaeron, where we ended up camped in front of the county Police HQ. This bode for either a quiet night or a very noisy one.

After a perfectly peaceful night and breakfast in the rain, we got away heading up towards Aberdovey and the offer of a decent night's accommodation at the Outward Bound centre. I knew Andy Jeffrey, the Head of Centre, and that reinforced by Fiona Whitehead's request had led to us being offered the use of the Centre and their Wharf Building to carry out any maintenance or sorting out we needed to do. It turned into quite a long, hot day, heading north past Aberystwyth and up to Borth. The beach from there to the entrance to the Aberdovey estuary was something of an interminable flog and as dire as I remembered it from years ago when I worked in Tywyn. However, all bad things come to an end and after we pulled in at the slip we were made very welcome. The boats ended up in the workshop, which was appropriate as I had by now knocked out both a knee hook (which gives the paddler control over the kayak) and my seat. They both needed regluing, which could only happen after the boat had been properly dried out. We were taken up to the Centre and given the use of the guest suites and, even better, the dining room facilities – a pleasant change from cooking over a single burner gas stove! It had been a good day, but the forecast was not promising and we were behind schedule. By now we had hoped to be on Anglesey, but the weather and the saints' heads had been against us from the start.

I had a dreadful night's sleep. I was obviously now too well attuned to sleeping in a tent and was moving rather slowly in the morning. Cath took one look at me and banned me from getting on the water. I did not argue. Instead we had an admin day, including a laundry run to Tywyn and lots of minor boat repairs. The wind got up very fiercely in the afternoon, reinforcing that not being on the water was a good idea. Cath was joined in the afternoon by her boyfriend, so they retired to a B&B, leaving me in sole occupancy of the guest quarters, not that I did much apart from fall on my bed and sleep very soundly indeed. Nine hours sleep and a good breakfast later, we all met up at the Wharf to be greeted by the sight of a flat tyre on the trolley. This turned out to be a catastrophic failure as the valve had torn away from the inner tube, something we could not fix ourselves. We were in the right place as Aberdovey has both a chandlers and a garage, but it was Sunday so everything came to life a little later than planned. We eventually got away in the murk and rain, and after a somewhat adventurous crossing of the harbour sandbar at the entrance to the estuary, we turned north and plodded up past Tywyn. This is not a very inspiring part of the coast at the best of times and was much less so in nil visibility and constant rain. Lunch was taken in the rain on a sandbank near Tonfannau, after which we kept well offshore of Barmouth, heading up towards Harlech. We saw many rafts of seabirds resting on the water, mostly manx shearwaters which was nice, and a lot of jet skis, which was less so. According to my diary, 'we plodded on until bored witless' (constant low-lying dunes with no backdrop in the rain and mist) and then turned right and landed through sporting surf. I got soaked. This was a sharp reminder to do up my collar before every landing and Cath had even worse fortune, getting trundled by a particularly aggressive wave. She rolled up and continued in but was very wet, and extremely cross. A short carry later, we hid from the wind in the dunes, hoping for better weather and lower surf in the morning.

The crossing of Tremadog Bay to the Tudwal islands was a real beauty. We got away in good order, although I did manage to get completely airborne off the back of two waves on the way out. On the way across, on a flat calm, glassy sea, we saw lots of shearwaters and divers, and came within hailing distance of a yacht making its way into the bay. They seemed a little surprised to see us seven miles from the nearest land, but it actually felt a very gentle and easy crossing, despite being 14 miles. Near the Tudwals, the sea got rather lumpy and we became the focus of attention of several jet skis out from the holiday camps. The steering ability of some of the drivers seemed less than good and they seemed determined to demonstrate the extent of their inability. Such behaviour left us short-tempered and rather cross as it was a similar feeling to being buzzed by motorbikes when pedalling a bicycle. After several trying minutes we got to a beach for lunch. The right side break was huge, but the middle was manageable with a bit of timing. Thereafter we continued along to and across Hell's Mouth. This was all a bit grim in fierce sunshine, but enlivened with a dolphin display as we went along. There were two or three of them, surging all around us and creating misty billows with their exhalations. Their speckled skins made for a fantastic show as they weaved around just under the surface of the sun-dappled sea. We thought about going into Aberdaeron on the south east side of the tip of the Lleyn peninsula but the surf was still running and it seemed a reasonable idea to use the tide to run through Bardsey Sound and get onto the north side. This plan worked well, right up to the western corner of the Sound, when a thick bank of mist and stiff northerly breeze hit us. The strength of the tide made it plain that retreat was not an option. A few scary minutes later, we broke out of the tide, into the lee of the cliffs, whereupon the wind dropped and things got a bit more reasonable. This allowed us to make good progress up to Porth Oer. The beach café was still open which meant that dinner became jacket potatoes with cheese and beans. Real food for once! The tents fitted neatly into two small alcoves at the end of the beach, each with a sea view and a perfect sunset. A pretty good end to long (30 mile) day. Although not entirely back on our planned schedule, we would at least arrive at the Symposium while the week of courses ran after the main weekend event.

To quote from my diary, the following day started a bit trying:

'Annoying headwind kept us inshore out of the tide and therefore into every reverse current known to man – and a few hitherto unknown!'

However, we got round the next headland into Porth Dinllaen, where the beach pub was open. This gave us a good excuse for lunch and refreshments. We generated lots of interest amongst the clientele, mainly of the 'you're mad, but good for you' variety. The next section of coast had some cliffs and pretty scenery, so we went a fair distance before finding a workable approach to the beach. This turned out to be a proper campsite, so we made use of the facilities before setting up home. Unfortunately the calculations revealed that we had to be on the water for 4 a.m. next day to catch the tide at the right moment to run through the Menai Straits. This was not a pleasant discovery. The consolation was that this meant we would be at the symposium site on Anglesey by lunchtime, giving us a couple of days off whilst we sorted out some minor problems with the boats. We would also meet up with a lot of our friends who were keen to see us. The start next morning was as horrible as we had feared, a long move to the water followed by a long paddle north. Sunrise over the mountains of North Wales is undoubtedly very pretty, but neither of us felt the need to see it too often. We were almost too tired to appreciate it. After a beach stop so that I could take my morning meds, we got to the entrance to the Strait. We had a bit of threading through sandbanks and their associated rough water before we got to the main channel. Here the flow picked up to seven knots, so we whizzed along passing Belan Fort at the entrance.

Once inside, and off Caernarvon, we made phone contact with Rick, the transport king at the symposium, arranging to be picked up somewhere between the Menai bridges and Beaumaris, depending on where we got to before the tide turned against us. This whole area was my old stamping ground from when I commanded the Joint Service Mountain Training Centre situated next to the bridge and it was nice to tick off all the markers as we made good progress. We got to Gallows Point just before Beaumaris before the wind and tide said 'no further' and then had a pleasant wait in the sun for Rick to arrive. Just before landing, we met up with an old friend, Loel Collins, working with a group from Plas y Brenin, the national outdoor activities centre. There were lots of smiles all around before they carried on with their trip, wishing us well with ours.

The big advantage of arriving at around midday at the symposium was – no people! This gave us sole use of the showers and dryers before the hordes returned so it was a pair of very clean and tidy paddlers who met their friends at the end of the afternoon. There were lots of greetings and reunions; it was really nice to be a part of it all, even if both of us were dog-tired. Martin Nissen, who had again driven from Denmark to be at the symposium, gave me a brand new paddle, especially selected and finished for strength, and Aled Williams, renowned boat designer, builder and paddler, spent an age finding and fixing an annoying leak in my rear hatch. Given that it was not one of his kayaks, that was really 'above and beyond the call of duty' and very much appreciated. And so to bed. We had been too tired to be sociable for too long, but the next two days would give us a chance to recharge our batteries, both electrical and mental.

Over the next two days we did a lot of admin and minor repairs. We had been going for 280 miles and just under a month. We knew what changes we wanted to make to the boats to fit them out the way we wanted after an extended 'road test'. The boats went to Nigel's factory for a keel strip on Cath's boat and to have four small D rings fibreglassed into the floor of the cockpits on both boats. When joined by thin elastic cord, the D rings provided a cradle under which we could stow pumps, sponges and anything else we needed quickly. Both deck bags were repaired at the Mouseloft, a sailmaker on the site at the symposium, and we managed to track down some beeswax zip lubricant for the zips on our suits. These were getting stiff from almost constant immersion in saltwater. Jen Kleck spent the afternoon sorting out the SPoT tracker account for me. (I found this a difficult process; in retrospect, I was a lot more tired at this stage than I had realised.) In the evening of the second day we all went out for dinner in Holyhead, and then retired to the tents amidst a mighty thunderstorm, which seemed to bounce around Holyhead Mountain for most of the night.

Taking stock of out adventure here was an interesting experience. I was engaged on the journey which had been born of a party at the symposium many years earlier and we were clearly admired and respected for our doing it, if not for the speed which we had so far managed. For myself, I was content with the way of life and Cath and I were getting on well, something which can never be taken for granted as people change when on extended expeditions and otherwise hidden personality traits can be revealed. The only niggling doubt was whether we were going to get all the way around in the time we had available. We would be fine if the weather stayed fair, but we did not need a repeat of our early days of being stuck on beaches while the wind and rain streamed over our tents. The weather, however, was not something we could control, so in many ways it was pointless to worry about it. Our plan was flexible and we had a good decision-making process in place between us, so we kept our fingers crossed for a good summer and autumn.

We could barely see the water at Gallows Point when Fiona returned us there, the tide was so far out. Launching was not feasible so we went back to Menai Bridge and launched there. This meant we had to repeat three or four miles, which led to a bit of muttering as we made our way along in drizzle and a cold wind. We crossed to the Great Orme using mainly the GPS as there was only limited visibility. Morale was not improved when the mist lifted to reveal thunder clouds boiling up over the North Wales mountains, spilling out towards us. Thunderstorms at sea are frightening and dangerous events as you are by default the highest thing around so the pace picked up (a lot) until we got under the Great Orme cliffs. Here we met another old friend, Pete Jones, out with a group, so we exchanged the time of day before heading around towards Llandudno. There was a lot of birdlife, and it was a really nice paddle. It was one which I had not done before and had been looking forward to. We passed under the pier whilst the 'end of the pier' show was in full swing but we could not pick out anywhere sensible to camp so moved across to the end of the beach just before the Little Orme cliffs. Here we camped at the top of the beach under some mock Victorian turrets, a quite bizarre background. It was nice to have a dry rear hatch again, but a shame I had clearly not quite closed the front hatch properly after lunch…

We woke to a fine, calm morning and set off around the Little Orme. This was, if anything, better than the Great Orme and a wonderful morning's paddle. From here on, life became rather less enjoyable as we carried on across the 'scenically challenged' section of North Wales' coast. Two interludes entertained us: we were waved at in mid-morning by three small figures who turned out to be the Danish contingent on their way home after the symposium, and a little later we watched a 'cops and robbers' scenario as two policemen attempted to collar some youths on the beach (for what, we did not know). Rhyll from seaward is an experience that need only be undertaken once, and the ice cream stop at Prestatyn failed to improve our opinion of there as well. Eventually we reached the Point of Air and made a long, long portage to the top of the beach in preparation for the Dee Estuary crossing in the morning. Because of the sand banks we needed to cross, we worked out that we would again have to be on the water at 4 a.m. to get the depth we needed. With that pleasant prospect in mind, we went to bed early but happy in the knowledge that with 315 miles under our keels, we had finished Wales.

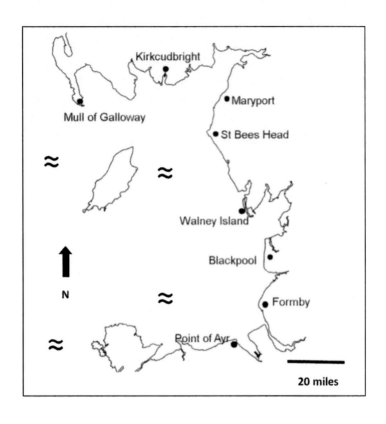

Map 3 - The West Coast of England and South West Scotland

'To Blackpool – and Beyond!'

12 May dawned sufficiently cold and clear to induce an asthma attack in Cath, leaving her struggling for breath as we prepared to launch. We had had a huge soft sand portage to get to the water and the exertion required from both of us certainly had something to do with it. Fortunately it responded to treatment from an inhaler and we were able to carry on. Life was not much better once we had launched, as we had a stiff four mile crossing at a fast pace across the banks of the Dee Estuary to get to Hilbre Island. It was very difficult to see until close to, as we were paddling directly into the early morning sun. The sun lay just above the horizon, right on our course, so there was no avoiding looking directly at it as we threaded our way across shallow banks leading to the north side of the estuary. Having had a quick break, in the mist at about 5.30 a.m., we carried on up the Mersey coast. We had lunch on the beach just north of the entrance to the channel into Liverpool and watched as the commando carrier HMS Bulwark came out. Thoughts of using the flood tide to push us up to Blackpool were discounted as we had already been up for a long time, so somewhere along the dunes of Formby, in the area of Sefton, it was 'right turn Clyde' and into the beach. We were rather wary about camping here as Steve Williams had had immense trouble when stuck here by weather on his attempted circumnavigation; so much so that he had christened Sefton 'The Land of No' because of all the signs saying 'no this, and no that'. Tucking into the base of the dunes, we reasoned

that we were not disturbing the dune flora and fauna and were causing less upset than the boy racers going up and down the beach in their cars. We were peered at by the crew of a Sefton Ranger Patrol vehicle, but nothing worse than that. We decided to get up a little early in the morning to get some of the tide. We did not fancy another very early start to get the full extent of the flow. That would still give us a long portage to the water, which we were not looking forward to at all… Whether it was a good thing or not, we could clearly see the Blackpool Tower – a full 20 miles to our north.

An early start preceded a long fight into a cold headwind; this was becoming a bit of an unpleasant habit. The coast was pretty uninteresting until the birdlife picked up off the Ribble Estuary but unfortunately the wind got up at the same time and proved somewhat trying. We were forced to keep close in as otherwise we would have been taken offshore very quickly. This led us to dance around the sandbanks and flats, nearly getting beached by the speed of the outflow at one stage. Having crossed the estuary, we took a very cold lunch break and from there carried on to and beyond Blackpool. This is another of those places I feel no urge to paddle by ever again. We took a beach break at one point, just after the Tower, and were buzzed by a jet ski. Cath and I were starting to think that our boats had a magnetic effect on these things. Unfortunately the driver misjudged his approach, hit a sandbank and went over the handlebars in a wonderfully spectacular fashion. Coming to the surface, unhurt but spluttering and somewhat crestfallen, he looked about to see if he his downfall had been observed. It had been and, sadly, we could not help laughing!

At Cleveleys lay the car ferry Riverdance, beached after a

The wreck of the Riverdance at Cleveleys. (C. Tanner)

storm in the February 2008 gales. Everyone got off safely but the refloating took so long that nature intervened and one night she fell on her side. Now she was just a shell, being broken up for scrap. Looking for somewhere to camp, we landed at a small beach about a mile further on, just where the flood defences became a continuous concrete embankment. The map showed an area of green behind the defences but it lied; the strip of green was just the edge of a road around a big housing estate, so camping on the beach became the answer, again. This was an interesting experience; local opinion was divided on whether we would be taken apart by feral gangs in the night, but always 'those from down there' – pointing in entirely opposite directions! There was a tribal feeling to the area. It turned out rather differently as people stopped by for a chat and brought us food and drink (entirely unbidden). One family took away all our electrics, with the promise of bringing them back charged before we set off the following morning. The night was relatively quiet with only one moped rider insisting on going backwards and forwards along the seawall. Fortunately he got bored before we did and disappeared off into the night.

I was up earlier than Cath the following morning as my choice of pitch was just a little too far down the beach for that tide and I had to do a spot of pre-breakfast relocating of my tent. True to their word, the family returned with our charged phones and radios, wished us well, and then waved us off as we headed across Morecambe Bay to the south west corner of the Lake District. We held position at the edge of the channel running in to the port of Fleetwood to allow three rather large and fast merchant ships to pass and also to allow a very rusty bucket to carry out what looked like a 3-point turn and go back into Fleetwood. A quick sprint across the channel then left us with a long, uneventful crossing to Walney Island. Lunch in the cold wind on an uninspiring sandbank was followed by a long slow section up the coast of Walney, looking for any potential campsite. Nothing much attracted, and quite a bit repelled, so we crossed Duddon Sands towards Haverigg Point. The crossing was wonderfully atmospheric, in clear evening light, but very, very cold. It was a relief to fight the stream on the north side and then set ourselves up on some gravel flats. According to the map, there was a prison just behind the dunes, but we never saw or heard anything of it.

Getting away from Haverigg was equally as sporting as landing there. The streams into Duddon Sands were in good form, giving us something of a fight to get round the corner and head north again. The next section proved a bit of a plod. The scale of the chart I was using was a little misleading and I kept on being given a sharp dose of 'positional reality' by the GPS. This was all very dispiriting. Just as we were about to cross Eskmeals Range, I spotted what must have been the smallest red flag ever, so we landed and I made contact with Range Control. After exchanging banter with the operator, who was also a sea paddler, we were cleared to cross and so made our way up to Ravenglass, which did look very pretty in the afternoon sunshine. We passed the nuclear reprocessing plant at Sellafield just as the range at Eskmeals let off an artillery round – that made us jump! At St Bees we camped on a shingle bench at the top of the beach with the compensation of a pub meal. This was very welcome as we had just about run out of the makings for lunches, and this day's had been particularly thin. We usually ate pasties (or pastries!), cheese and either bagels or pitta bread.

These all have a limited life span in a kayak and even with our willingness to eat around any mould, we needed to resupply regularly. Our plan was to find a shop in the morning and then set ourselves up for a crossing of the Solway Firth the day after. My diary noted that 'a shower would be greatly appreciated!'

We got away from St Bees in good order, passing the first of the Heads on our way north. The birdlife was spectacular with lines of razorbills and guillemots filling every ledge with black and white. Columns of birds flew outwards and inwards as they went to feed or returned with fish for their young. In retrospect, this turned out to be the best section of the English west coast between Wales and Scotland. Getting into Whitehaven was easy as the lock gate was open. Getting out, after we found out that it was easier to get to Tesco's from the beach outside the harbour, was less so. The lock gate was closed, so I climbed a ladder to make contact. The lockkeeper had not seen us come in and was 'unhappy'. Quite why it was my fault he had not seen us, I was never sure. After a serious and lengthy moan, we were told to wait for two yachts to enter the lock, after which we were grudgingly allowed out. On a lighter note, we chatted at the back of the harbour to two of the local hard men – all T shirts (in the cold and rain) and tattoos. Sadly the image was rather spoilt by the fact that both of them had bejewelled chihuahuas on leads, a hilariously incongruous sight! Leaving the boats on the beach, we visited Tesco's and then had the usual nightmare of cramming everything into the boats. This was one of the easiest points of access we had to any supermarket anywhere around the coast. Back on the water, we experienced the delights of paddling the industrial wasteland coast of west Cumbria with its cliffs of eroded slag and waste piles. This is not a pretty section of the coast. Arriving at Workington, we again opted for the 'top of the beach' option. We hoped that this would put us in a good position to cross the Solway Firth to Kirkcudbright if the weather played fair. Even better news was that Colin McWilliams, a friend from Oban, had contacted Kirkcudbright Range Control and found out that there was no firing over the weekend. That meant we could get a clear run along the ranges, rather than lose a week or have to paddle at some odd time when the ranges paused. Scotland and the Isle of Man were clearly visible in the evening light.

They were not visible in the morning. Low grey cloud, rain, a cold wind and poor visibility were our companions as we set off on the crossing. Two miles later the seas had built up to such an extent that those on landing on the far side would have been huge. It was plain we were being over-adventurous (if not downright silly), so we turned and battled the wind back to the Cumbrian coast. A horrible slog then ensued as we clawed our way to Maryport, where we ended up on a corner of a beach vying for the award of the most horrible campsite so far. We were cold and edgy after the attempt at the crossing, and camping on an industrial wasteland did not help to calm us very much. However, looking over a low wall at the top of the embankment behind us changed life considerably – there was a marina! Putting on my best 'blagging' face, I went to the reception and deployed 'full charm'… It must have worked, because we ended up being allowed to use the showers, washing machines and driers, and to charge our electrics. Cath's face was a picture when I got back to the tents with the news. Life improved again when two friends, Jim and Sue Savege, visited us in the afternoon. I think the cups of tea I made were rather poor exchange for bags of fruit and bottles of ginger beer. (Well, that's what the look on Sue's face conveyed!) Passers-by warned us in doom-laden tones that we were camped where 'the kids come down to hang about', but there were not that many options and by late afternoon we certainly were not moving that day. True to form, a group did turn up at about 9 p.m., already fully in party mode and with a plentiful supply of bottles to keep themselves topped up. A few comments were exchanged, all friendly, and they went around the corner to have their bonfire there. As the wind was blowing away from us, there was absolutely no problem for us. One lad on a mountain bike decided to buzz the tents a few times, but he got bored before we did, leaving us to a reasonably quiet night.

We awoke to a gloriously sunny morning, with a gentle breeze at our backs, so it was up and away to Scotland. Four and a half hours later, we scrambled to make a quick landfall for a break as a leg stretch was definitely needed. The outgoing stream was running at a fair rate, making the boulder beach landing somewhat tricky. Thereafter it was off with the tide, running along the Solway coast and the Kirkcudbright range wall. This is a superb stretch of coast, an undeclared little gem with cliffs, caves, arches, reefs and islets. All in all, a sea kayaker's paradise. There were little bumps off all the points, but nothing to disturb us too much. The scenery was spectacular and we took an inordinate number of pictures on this stretch. Passing lots of seals, we crossed Kirkcudbright Bay and pulled in to the bay east of Dundrod Point. After 24 miles we were glad to be off the water and finding a 'trolley-friendly' slip was a real bonus. The map showed that we were on the edge of a proper campsite, so I walked miles (at least it felt like it!) to find reception and check it was alright for us to camp at the top of the slip. Indeed it was and the proprietor not only drove me back to the boats but told us to use the showers and anything else we wanted, absolutely free. Cath's face was again a picture; I think she was starting to think I had some magic dust I was sprinkling over people. After showering, we had a go at fixing the leak which had developed around Cath's skeg box. This turned out to be a major problem and needed looking at by someone with more tools to hand than we were carrying. I made contact with Aled and he agreed to come and meet us in Luce Bay, to repeat the magic he had done with my boat. By this stage it was the 18th of May; we had done 435 miles, and reached Scotland, so we were rather pleased at our progress.

IN MEMORY OF THE LOCAL MEN WHO DIED AT THE SINKING OF THE
FISHING VESSEL "SOLWAY HARVESTER" OFF THE SOUTH-EAST COAST
OF THE ISLE-OF-MAN ON THE 8th JANUARY 2000

Robin Scott Mills   aged 33 years
Andrew Craig Mills   aged 29 years
Martin Hugh Milligan   aged 26 years
John Doyle Murphy   aged 22 years
David Mills   aged 18 years
Wesley John Jolly   aged 17 years
David Joseph Lyons   aged 17 years

ERECTED BY THE FREEMASONS

The 'Solway Harvester' memorial.

Terra Incognita – South West Scotland

The next section of the Solway coast, west towards Luce Bay, passed reasonably uneventfully; there were some frisky moments off the points and heads, but in the main we went with the flow and admired the scenery. We had a short break at one stage and discovered that we were on the small headland at Kinghorn where a memorial to the crew of the fishing vessel Solway Harvester had been placed. Solway Harvester was a local scallop boat lost whilst working off the Isle of Man in a storm in January 2000. There was initially thought that her nets had been snagged by a submarine and the boat dragged under, but a Marine Accident Investigation found that poor maintenance and lack of safety equipment had led to her loss with all seven crewmen on board. The afternoon was a bit more of a fight as the tide had turned against us and there was now only a boulder beach to admire in passing… All things come to an end, and we pulled in to a beach just inside the east edge of Luce Bay. The crossing to the Mull of Galloway looked very inviting in the evening light, but we had already done 23 miles that day, and the thought of another 12 miles in the gathering gloom was probably not a sensible option. We also needed to meet up with Aled to get Cath's leaking skeg box fixed, so camping next to the 5th tee of the local golf course became the answer. Had we known that we were to spend the next week getting to the Mull of Galloway, we might have made a different decision, but nine continuous days on the go were taking their toll, and a night landing in the area of the Mull of Galloway seemed a little over-adventurous. We woke to a cold wind, and the greens keeper giving our patch of rough a bit of a strim; perhaps it was a none too subtle hint to shift? We hid from the wind all the way down the coast to Auchenmalg, whereat lay the campsite we had arranged to meet Aled. An adventurous boulder landing got us ashore, but as the wind was by now very cold (where was summer?) we decided to have lunch in the pub before sorting out camping. The Cock Inn must vie for being the weirdest pub in the country. We decided that it was run by the relatives of the Munsters (you need to be of my vintage to remember the black and white TV programme about a family of vampires) and the décor was something else, but the baked potatoes made up for the bizarre atmosphere!

After lunch, I walked to the campsite. As I got closer, there seemed to be an alarming lack of tents and an overabundance of fixed caravans. Things did not look good; and so it turned out – the site had been 'caravan only' for three years, and they did not take tents. Even my most mournful looks seemed to be falling on deaf ears until Laura (the wife of the owner) rang her husband and convinced him that an exception could be made for us. Things started to look up and then suddenly became even better as it was decided that we could use the spare caravan used for staff 'in the season'. All of a sudden I was being given the tour of a really smart caravan (TV, fridge, showers etc) and told 'because of what you're doing, you can have it for free'; words truly failed me! Once again, the look on Cath's face as I introduced her to where we were 'going to pitch the tents' was an absolute picture. Recovering rapidly from the surprise, we got organised and started the cleaning process. Aled would come to find us next day, and we would have a good chance of a proper rest before crossing the back of Luce Bay and moving up to the Mull of Galloway.

The day off was very welcome after 10 long days on the water; we got lots of small repairs and adjustments done, and Aled arrived in the afternoon to deal with Cath's boat. As with mine earlier in the trip, one too many bangs on the hull in the area of the skeg box had caused a crack, allowing water to get in around the box. Temporary repairs had coped initially, but it needed to be looked at sooner rather than later. This turned out to be a bigger job than any of us had thought as the crack was extensive and deep and needed the full range of Aled's box of tricks to fix. It was a full four hours before a sense of humour was restored to all concerned. Another bizarre pub meal closed the day, after which Aled made a very belated trip back to Penrith. The next day started with the embarrassing realisation that we were beached by wind. We could not have got off the beach against what was coming in, let alone made progress against it. And it was bitterly cold again. Laura kindly allowed us an extension of one more night, and then her husband gave us the use of a van to go into Stranraer because there were no buses that day. Again, we were overwhelmed by the generosity of people who helped us enormously for no other reason than that we were there.

Shopping in Stranraer gave rise to one of those weird coincidences; I turned around in the supermarket checkout queue to find myself face-to-face with Franco Ferrero – an old friend who was on a yachting trip with his brother. They had intended to be further north by this stage but conditions 'outside' had proved to be too sporting, so they had run for shelter into Stranraer. It is truly a small world. We returned to the campsite, where we had a large meal and then hid from the rain which was falling heavily but vertically. At last the wind had dropped.

The problem with Luce Bay is the RAF. To explain, there is a bombing range down the middle of the bay, with the targetry at the inshore end. Unhelpfully, every attempt at finding out whether the range was 'live' or not were frustrated by answerphone messages that were unintelligible and by contact phone numbers which went unanswered. As a result, it was with some trepidation that we launched and then had a 'long sprint' across the back of the bay. Stress levels were raised a couple of times by flashes from seaward which might have been the nose lights of aircraft (but were probably just sunlight off the buoys). It was good to get ashore on the far side for a rest and at least here we got reasonable shelter from the wind, which had again got up. And so at the end of the afternoon we landed at Drummore. We had missed the tide for rounding the Mull that evening and this at least gave us access to the village for another pub meal. We camped on an ivy mat at the back of the beach underneath, as it turned out, a sign on the path above which read 'Area subject to landslip' – ignorance is bliss! Walking around Drummore took all of six minutes as it is both pretty and pretty small, so we had a drink and retired to the tents. Fingers were crossed for the forecast to improve but the evening one had not been too promising.

Bank Holiday Saturday, 24 May, dawned bright, sunny and extremely windy. The bay was a mass of whitecaps; we were beached again. Frustrating, in fact very frustrating, but something we just had to work around. We could not get round the Mull of Galloway in these conditions, so we had to think long term. A quiet day followed; breakfast in the café was followed by, after a suitable interval, a meal in the pub in the evening. We left just before the 'noted artiste, Roxanne' started to perform... Sunday was no better and probably even windier. The highlight of the day was being adopted by Rena and Alex, a couple who lived in the house right behind us. We were invited to come in for a shower, hopefully not because the smell was drifting up from our camp. Lots of reading, small admin and Sudoku gets done on days like this. In fact, on a trip hit by bad weather, the amount of reading done is quite astonishing and one of our minor problems became book exchanges. Fortunately our taste in reading matter was mostly compatible...

Another windy day followed and we were invited to attend Rena's house, carrying any washing that needed doing. I am not sure her washing machine will recover, but it was a very welcome event. Washing mainly consisted of either cold water in the little collapsible bowl, or finding a convenient sink in a public toilet. We were entertained all morning and then, after lunch, taken up to the Mull for a look around. Coincidentally we were going through the same process as another would-be-circumnavigator who had been stuck at Drummore for a week the previous year. Our reconnaissance revealed the existence of an inside line, which was very reassuring as the offshore action was rather spectacular with extensive areas of wildly confused water which was not anything we wanted to get involved with. Then it was off to visit Port Logan, the next village on the outside of the Mull, and the setting for the TV series '2000 Acres of Sky'. It was weird looking around and going 'recognise that, recognise there...' despite never having actually been there. In the evening we did some tidal planning. Alex is an ex-Navy officer, with extensive local tidal knowledge, so it was nice to know that our and his tidal calculations agreed. So it was off to bed with fingers and toes crossed for a good day tomorrow; although Drummore was nice, we did not need to be stuck there any longer.

The next 12 miles were scary… The Mull of Galloway is a significant tongue of land sticking out into an area of fast flowing water; as a result, there is always 'something going on', even on calm days. The whole volume of the Irish Sea passes the Mull in both directions twice a day with the tide and the Mull sticking out into this flow has a result akin to putting a finger across the spout of a tap at full power. The same amount of water comes out but at much greater speed. Imagine the tap turned on its side and it is easy to see why we wanted to be at the Mull when the tap was at a dribble rather than at full throttle. With my usual enthusiasm for being 'early', we were up and away on time and then got to the bay before the Mull about an hour ahead of time. The sensible, indeed planned, option would have been to wait for the hour and then go at slack water. But it was cold and raining, so we went early… This of course led us to get severely chastised in the tide race before the point. Turning round and getting out of it proved unpleasant, and it was a 'gently shaken, not stirred' pair of paddlers who regrouped in the bay to think things through. We moved the boats above the tide line and decided to walk up to the Mull to have another look. This took a while, and of course the tide had calmed down by then and the passage was eminently 'go-able'. We had a quick cup of tea and returned to the boats for another attempt. This again took a while, so of course we now arrived at the point as the tide was in full flow… To say that the next few minutes were 'full on' would be understating it quite a lot. At one point I dropped into a hole created in the water when the sea rebounded in all directions. I was behind some rocks and had an extreme 'bracing skills workout' to stay upright, with Cath behind me hoping I would not need rescuing because she was similarly engaged. After several minutes threading between fangs of rocks surrounded by chaotic white water, our paddles flashing in all directions and our bodies moving instinctively to keep us upright, we at last pulled beyond the point and onto the outside of the Mull. Things now calmed down a lot. The inside passage north was straightforward and relatively benign compared to the action going on offshore. The inshore eddies were against us, but at least we got some shelter from the wind, which nonetheless still came over the cliffs and hammered us from time to time.

We aimed for Port Logan but I became very tired a few miles short and we pulled in to Clanyard Bay. This would be very scenic if not for all the rubbish which accumulates here, mostly, it would seem, from the rubbish tips in Belfast. Anyway, we put the tents up in constant drizzle and no wind. As a consequence of the lack of wind we got midges instead. We did an adventurous cliff walk in the evening, attempting to get a phone signal, but had no luck. Hopefully the SPoT had done its job and people knew we were ashore safe. At about 9 p.m. we were hit by two tremendous gusts of wind, prompting me to get out and peg down the additional storm guys. As I climbed out of the tent, I realised Cath was in trouble: the gusts had collapsed her tent, breaking a pole in the process, and then rolled her over, through a thistle patch, wrapping her in the tent outer and inner at the same time. She was now wrapped up like a mummy, calling for help and stuck! I could not help laughing as I rescued her from the wreckage. Sorting it all out took a while, and we then spent a lot of time finding planks of wood and big boulders to stormproof her tent. Finally to bed – and we enjoyed an entirely quiet, wind free night…!

We passed Portpatrick the following day, stopping for a café lunch as it rained hard all day. Fortunately the owner did not mind us dripping all over his floor. The afternoon passed in the same rain and a rising wind, so we did not get to the north end of the Rhinns as we had hoped, but still made 20 miles, camping in a sodden boulder field about two miles short. The day was a significant day; I was now on my longest sea kayak expedition as we had covered 513 miles in total. My previous longest trip had been around the Queen Charlotte Islands in British Columbia, a total of 506 miles.

The wind dropped overnight, and the rain stopped too. Unfortunately we then attracted the midges. Lots and lots of them. Midges are an irritant well known to anyone who has visited Scotland in their season (which, with milder winters, is now close to being all year round). Near invisible, they find any gaps in clothing in their desire to settle on the skin and feed on your blood. The resulting bite is remarkably itchy and can drive sufferers to distraction. Getting off the beach was a welcome relief, but some little beasts managed to hitchhike for quite a distance. We passed the lighthouse in glorious sunshine and then sat at the cardinal mark at the entrance to Loch Ryan, working out when to cross the ferry lane to get to the other shore. It was very busy, but eventually a suitable window opened, so we sprinted the mile across. We had been monitoring Channel 14 on the VHF, the port operations channel, and heard the inbound vessel behind which we had crossed warning the outbound ferry of our presence. I then had a conversation with the outbound skipper, assuring him that we were well out of his way! He picked us out at a range of at least a mile, so his bridge binoculars must have been impressively powerful. During the crossing I managed to scare Cath quite badly; having paddled over a huge jellyfish, I remarked 'Wow, that's a big one!' She thought I had spotted yet another fast ferry and was not best pleased to discover that I was only getting excited about a jellyfish!

We then had a long hot paddle up to Girvan thinking that perhaps summer had finally appeared. The scenery was nice up to Lendalfoot, but 'average' thereafter although lots of seals basked in the sunshine. Arriving in Girvan, we made contact with Ann and Geoff Turner of the kayaking firm Karitek, and they came to pick us up for a night in their house – and an enormous meal. The forecast was at last showing a period of decent weather, so we hoped to cross to Arran the following day and perhaps even get to the Mull of Kintyre the day after.

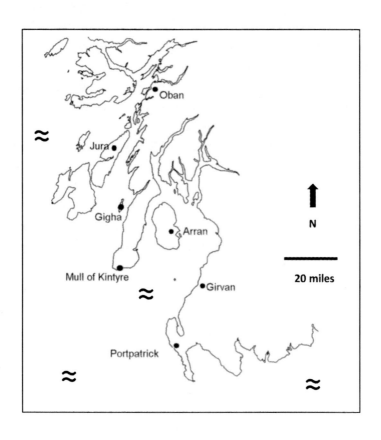

Map 4 – Home Waters – West Coast Scotland

Home Waters

Sleeping in a house did not seem to agree with us; we both felt a bit 'different' from sleeping inside and had obviously become seriously adapted to the outdoor life. For me, it felt airless being inside, even with the window open, and I went through my usual 'sleep badly on the first night in a strange place' routine. Ann built us a huge breakfast then ran us back to Girvan, stopping for a supermarket reload on the way. The weather had really improved, and packing the boats was hot work. Then it was off on a direct crossing to Pladda, a little island just off the south tip of Arran. The last four miles of the 15 were really hard work for me. I had a seriously unpleasant headache, probably from the combined effects of a poor night's sleep and too much sun on the back of my neck. I was dehydrated and nearly vomiting for the last hour – no fun at all. Cath played a starring role looking after me and getting me ashore on the island, where I then sat around until I felt half human again. When I could appreciate it, Pladda turned out to be a little gem. We had two nice pitches for the tents, magical scenery and an abundance of birdlife. During the crossing, I had been very conscious of naval anti-submarine warfare exercises going on. A frigate was running around 'sprinting then listening' and we were very glad when the combination disappeared off round the outside of Ailsa Craig. Equanimity was further disturbed in the evening when we saw a fast-cat ferry passing the Girvan coast, inbound to Glasgow. Until then, we had no idea that we had crossed a fast-ferry route.

It was a noisy night as the gulls and oystercatchers seemed to be very light sleepers, and dawn came far too early. On the plus side, it was a calm, blue sky day, so passing along the south coast of Arran was really enjoyable. The nine mile crossing to Campbeltown started well, but half way across a nasty headwind kicked in and the whole thing became an unpleasant struggle in a pronounced chop. Cath was cold and very tired by the time we got to the far side, so we moved onto the mainland shore to a sheltered beach where she took two hours out to sleep and recover. Afterwards we gently aquarambled along the coast towards the Mull of Kintyre, stopping on what appeared to be a perfect beach at the quaintly named Arranman's Barrels. Appearances can be deceptive however... What we had not appreciated was that we were in fact on the outskirts of a huge caravan site, and it was Saturday night. All went well until a female voice at 2 a.m. announced 'I've found a canoe!' So she had, and found a very cross owner too. The group then went to the other end of the beach and were marginally less noisy, only returning to apologise for disturbing us! Not our best night and one of the reasons we developed an immutable law: 'on Friday and Saturday nights, camp miles from anywhere.'

Rounding the Mull of Kintyre turned out to be one of the finest paddling days we had ever had. The Mull has a strong and justifiable reputation for frightening experiences amongst sea kayakers and small craft skippers. It is another

The lighthouse at the Mull of Kintyre.

of those 'fingers across the tap' locations but here the width of the Irish Sea is at its least with only 12 miles separating Scotland and Ireland. As a result, there is rarely if ever a true period of slack water; something is always moving. As a result, it is an incautious kayaker who does not carefully plan their passage around the Mull of Kintyre. On our day we woke to a blue sky and flat seas. I have to confess that we did absolutely no tidal planning whatsoever, we just got up and went. At the back of my mind was the thought that we could always hop the back eddies if the tide was against us. In reality, there were no back eddies as the streams run close to the rocks and cliffs, so a contra-tide run probably is not possible. Fortuitously we had strong streams running in our favour as we admired the stunning cliff scenery. It was a superb day, but totally committing. If anything went wrong with the weather, there would be nowhere to hide for about 14 miles. We stopped in Machrihanish for a celebratory (late) pub lunch and the steak burgers went down very well. Then we crossed Machrihanish Bay in an evil NE wind, which knocked our speed down a lot. To compound the fun, the rain started as well. As a result we stopped in Port Crom, a bit short of our 'best effort' target of a night on Gigha, but a good beach site. The midges and drizzle encouraged us to get the tents up quickly, and after a good meal we retired, basking in the glow of a very good day.

Well, if the previous day had been good, the next turned out even better, once we had escaped the midges which seemed to come in partnership with the calm, settled weather. We crossed to Gigha, taking a break and getting an ice cream, and then 'went with the flow' across West Loch Tarbet and up towards Loch Sween. From here on in, I was effectively on home ground. The whole day was spent on a flat sea, with stunning views across the Sound of Jura towards Islay and Jura. We stopped after 30 miles in a small nook and cranny four miles short of Carsaig Bay. We escaped the midges by cooking and eating on the rock shelves, only going onto the marsh grass when we really had to. Any thoughts of an early night were lost as we settled down to watch a perfect sunset over Jura's hills, known from their symmetry and shape as 'The Paps'. It is a good job that cameras these days are digital; I dread to think how many rolls of 35 mm film I would have shot that night.

The morning midges chivvied us off the beach and into a fast running northbound stream. We rode this up to the gap between the islands and the tip of the Craignish Peninsula, known as the Dorus Mor from the Gaelic for 'Great Door'. The tide accelerates through this gap, shooting out in a fast jet of water pointed straight at the Gulf of Corryvreckan between the islands of Jura and Scarba. Although on a 'normal' paddling day we would gladly have embraced the challenge of Corryvreckan with its fierce tides and whirlpools, today we had more basic delights in mind as Oban, home, lay only a few more miles to the north. Having passed through the Dorus Mor, admiring the seals lazily swimming around and under us, we crossed towards the Sound of Luing, between Luing and Scarba. The Gulf of Corryvreckan passed on our left, followed quickly afterwards by the Pass of the Grey Dogs at the top of Scarba. Known colloquially to sea kayakers as 'Grey Dogs', the channel gets its name from an incident in history when a small vessel carrying two people and two grey dogs, traditionally thought to be deerhounds, was lost in the whirlpools and wild waters of the constricted channel. According to which interpretation you prefer, the name was given because the dogs survived and the people did not, or alternatively the people survived and the dogs did not.

Whichever the correct version of the tale, here it got extremely windy for a bit, making the seas quite lively and us quite cold. We passed Belnahua doing 10.2 knots on the GPS – unfortunately I didn't manage to get a picture of the readout as I was a bit busy at the time… Belnahua and Easdale are known as the 'Islands that roofed the world' because of their extensive slate quarries from which thousands of tons of slate were extracted to be shipped across the world for roof tiles. Both quarries succumbed to the sea, Easdale's in a spectacular fashion after the perimeter wall was breached by a storm in the night and Belnahua's more prosaically when a damp seam was found, slowly filling the workings with sea water. No lives were lost in either case. By the time we got to the north end of Seil Island, we were both becoming tired, but the lure of Oban, home, was upon us, so after a quick lunch overlooking the lump of rock known to local seafarers as Dragon Island from its profile viewed from the west, we rode the southerly swell into the Sound of Kerrera. Neither of us had the puff to pass Oban and paddle right to Connel, so we pulled in to Puffin Dive, a dive centre situated just south of Oban in the Sound of Kerrera. We were met by Carol and then taken home for a hard-earned two days off before starting the next leg up to the very tip of Scotland. Another 30 mile day, making our trip total so far 656 miles in 51 days.

The plan was to spend no more than two days at home. Any longer and we reckoned we would lose the impetus to go on. The Wednesday was spent on an orgy of washing, cleaning and kit maintenance. My diary notes that I ended the day 'tired – but clean!' Thursday passed in a similar vein with food and equipment shopping, and then final preparations for the resumption of the trip on Friday. The tides were in our favour; we could have a leisurely start and catch the flow northbound through the Sound of Mull.

Passing Belnahua at over 10 knots.

A good drying day.

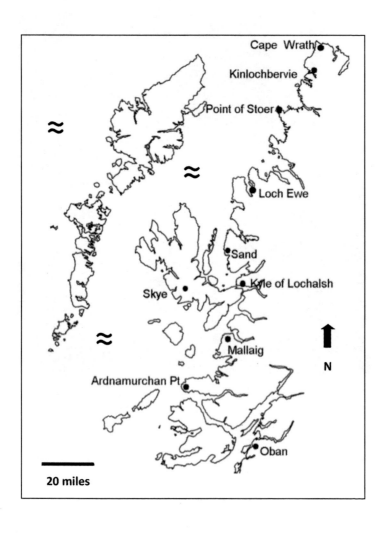

Map 5 – North West Scotland

Cath and Rowland at the boat launch, April 2008.

Day 2 - across the Bristol Channel.

Off the entrance to the River Mersey.

Mirror seas.

In the Sound of Jura.

Looking to the Small Isles from Ardnamurchan.

West coast weather - Point of Stoer.

Return to Cape Wrath - probably not what the cardiologist had in mind!

One of the many storms that hit us in California.

What seemed like a perfect evening at Aldeburgh…

…and what faced us the following morning.

Waiting for the sea to return in Foulness Ranges.

Our second night run down the Essex coast.

The third corner – North Foreland in Kent.

Dungeness, after the storm.

A long landing in west Sussex.

Up to the Corner

Getting going was easy in some respects, but the farewell was as trying as ever. We moved up the Sound of Kerrera under a grey but quiet sky then turned to the north west and the entrance to the Sound of Mull. Crossing to Lismore was straightforward, but the wind and rain paid us a visit, making us quite cold as we lunched looking at Lismore Light. Then followed a quick dash across to Lady's Light, not quite playing 'chicken' with the ferry to the Hebrides, and on to Mull. Lady's Light got its name after an incident in 1527. The sister of the Earl of Argyll, Lady Catherine Campbell, was married to Lachlan Maclean of Duart (on Mull). One night he rowed his wife from the castle on Mull to the rock and left her there at low tide. Observing the following morning that there was no sign of her, he sent a message to the Earl of Argyll in Inverary, saying that he would return Lady Catherine's body for burial with her family. On arriving in Inverary, with a cortege and coffin, Maclean was escorted to the great hall for refreshments, only to discover his 'drowned' wife at the head of the table, next to her brother. (She had been rescued from the rock, by a supporter, during the night.) Nothing was said of the incident and Maclean was allowed to leave Inverary albeit without his wife. He was, however, murdered in his bed whilst in Edinburgh a little while later by Lady Catherine's brother. 'Serve's him right!' was Cath's comment.

Going up the sound of Mull, we had the tide with us, but a

headwind kicked in so we stopped after 15 miles at the ferry crossing to Lochaline. This gave us a nice pitch, if a somewhat challenging landing with heavy boats. The weather cleared and the forecast seemed favourable for a good day ahead. The next morning was still and clear, apart from the legions of midges. Quite a few ended up in my porridge and Cath's noodles and we did not lose some hitchhikers for about an hour on the water. The passage up to Tobermory was idyllic with absolutely flat calm seas, mountains in the background and the occasional bank of early morning mist rolling across the Sound. We succumbed, inevitably, to the lure of pies and ice creams in Tobermory and then followed the coast northwards until we crossed to the south side of the Ardnamurchan peninsula. This was unpleasant in an evil beam wind and seas, so it was a relief when the conditions improved greatly on the Ardnamurchan side. There are not very many camp spots south of the Point, so we pressed on. We were aiming to get round the westernmost point on the British mainland and end up looking across to the Small Isles and the area up towards Arisaig. This turned out to be a magical afternoon and evening. We saw a basking shark along the Ardnamurchan north shore and spent a few minutes watching this magnificent creature lazily moving to and fro, sifting plankton through its gills to feed. Basking sharks have made a successful comeback in these waters after a period in the 1960s and 1970s when they were all but wiped out by extensive shark fishing. We then found a beautiful site on a sandy bay to camp for the night. The views across to Rhum, Eigg and up to Arisaig were stunning; it was another evening spent taking many pictures. We had both settled back quickly into 'expedition mode', and were looking forward to making good progress up to the north coast.

It rained in the night, but held off as we packed the boats and left for 'Mallaig and beyond'. Cath nearly had an unplanned aquatic moment on the very first reef, but after that everything settled down and we had another spectacular paddle in superb wilderness and stunning views. Off the entrance to Arisaig, we came across a guided group of day paddlers. Some of them looked distinctly unhappy about where they had been placed whilst the rest of the group played around a reef break, and it seemed to be a case of too many students to one instructor. We passed them quickly and got up towards Arisaig itself. Here we had our first (and as it turned out, only) nude sunbather sighting. Sadly, for me, it was a chap! The Arisaig island chain is beautiful but we passed it all too quickly. The rest of the coast up to Mallaig is not of the same scenic quality as quite a lot of it is sea defence concrete and blocks to protect the new road. It being by now a little late, we decided to have fish and chips in Mallaig before moving on to find a campsite a little further north. After sitting and watching an otter at the entrance to Mallaig harbour, we crossed to Knoydart and eventually got ashore in Doune Bay near a set of cabins and lodges that were distinctly Alaskan in appearance. The wind kept the midges down, but sadly did nothing about the deer ticks, which seemed abundant in our chosen campsite.

The next day dawned horribly with strong winds and driving rain so we were beached again. This was not an unfamiliar feeling. We made contact with the owner of the Lodge and arranged to have a shower, well worth the £2 per head, and were allowed to recharge all our electrics in the afternoon when the generator was running. It was largely a quiet day, punctuated by the frequent removal of ticks from various parts of our anatomies.

We were up and away early, but the wind increased and we had to deal with a horrible quartering sea in front of a Force 6-7 wind. This was not fun, so we turned – or skidded – round into the entrance to Loch Hourn and found a small storm beach to camp on. We were 'tents up and organised' by 1030 in the morning! We explored the coast in between rather heavy showers, finding a stag skull at one point. One antler had been broken, but the other was in good condition, so the hacksaw came into play for another souvenir of the trip. Frustratingly, Gordon Brown, friend, paddler, coach and owner of Skyak Adventures, who lived on the Skye shore almost opposite us, was offering the use of his hot tub – but crossing to the Skye shore was out of the question. The evening was still windy, but the forecast had us hoping to get away in the morning. It would be good to go as there were a lot of ticks on this beach too.

We did get away, and caught a decent flow through the Kylerhea narrows, watching lots of seals as we 'went with the flow'. Kylerhea is the 'secret passage' inside Skye and allows mariners to avoid the often dangerous coastline of the west coast of Skye. It is also a much shorter route to northern waters. The payment extracted by Nature for these advantages is the greatly increased flow through the narrows, with flows of over 10 knots not being unknown. Fortunately, Nature smiled, if somewhat damply, on our passage and it was fast and flat. Thereafter the weather deteriorated and our first sight of the Skye Bridge was through a veil of driving cold rain. As a consolation, a school of dolphins preceded us, giving an impressive display of aquabatics as they went. We stopped at the Kyle of Lochalsh to restock in the Co-op, attracting a lot of tourist attention as we did so. We also exchanged pleasantries with the Leopard Man, a tattooed eccentric, living in a ruin on the Skye shore, who also used a kayak to do his shopping. Tom Leppard has spent in excess of £5000 on tattoos which cover his entire body with leopard spots and markings. He is an ex-special forces soldier who had, at the time we met him, eschewed a 'normal' lifestyle and lived in a bothy on the shore of Skye near Kyleakin. Every week or so he would paddle across to Kyle of Lochalsh to buy his groceries and collect his pension. As at the date of writing this, 2013, he has finally succumbed to civilisation and lives in a house in Broadford on Skye.

After lunch we passed under the bridge and crossed Loch Carron in the teeth of a rising headwind. That was not any fun at all and we were very glad to get into shelter on the far side. We passed the Crowlins and eventually ran out of steam just short of Camusteel. It was a bit awkward finding somewhere sensible to get off the water, but we at last found a tiny beach in Poll Domhain. As a consolation, we even managed to get intermittent phone reception whilst standing on a small hillock near the tents, so contact could be made with home.

We got away next morning into the teeth of a horrible headwind. We plugged along the coast and got into Applecross bay. Any hope of camping there was quickly dismissed, so we moved on again to a bay marked 'Sand' on the map, two miles further north. As we pulled into the beach, a huge black dog came running down the sands and threw itself into the edge of the surf, barking furiously. Not entirely convinced by the wagging tail, I kept a firm grip on my paddle as I got out of the boat! Looking up again, I saw a tall man now running across to us. This generated thoughts of 'here we go, you can't camp here'. But it was not to be. The figure was Monty Halls, an ex-Royal Marine now a TV star, who was in the process of 'living the crofter dream' – Beachcomber Cottage. (He has subsequently done a TV series from Ireland, and another one from the Cornish fishing village of Cadgewith.) He was doing the whole self-sufficiency bit with boar, chickens, kitchen garden, Soay sheep and solar panels! This was a marked contrast to the lifestyle of the previous hermit, Tom Leppard, we had met in Kyle of Lochalsh… We were welcomed in by Monty and Reubs the dog, if not by the producer of the series, and set up camp by the sheepfold. It turned out that we were not entirely 'out of shot', if you saw the series… We had a pleasant explore in the afternoon, and finally retired after doing our bit and rounding up the chickens. Unexpectedly, the wind pinned us down for the next two days, so we got to know Monty, Reubs, the cottage and the local area reasonably well. To quote from my diary:

'Dog-sat, entertained visitors, went for a hill walk (collecting many ticks), and then sat and listened to the Archers! All part of the ongoing lesson in patience which is an expedition.'

On the second day we went to Applecross and spent some time in the café and pub writing postcards before returning to yet more intermittent views across to Skye. Rounding up the chickens that evening was unnecessarily exciting as the cockerel's flight feathers were growing and he did a runner, nearly being caught and eaten by one of the boar. The consolation of battling again into the wind the next day was threefold as we had eagle sightings, otter sightings and a nice campsite in Red Point bay, 12 miles further up the coast. We were both getting fed up with paddling into the headwinds; where had summer gone?

Perhaps the wind gods heard us, because the next morning (the middle of June), the winds were from the southwest. They were also Force 5, so we had a lumpy passage up the coast, past Melvaig and around and across Loch Ewe. It then started to pick up, and swung into our faces, so we crashed into Opinan Bay, giving ourselves the portage from hell to get across the boulders to the grass. By the time we finished both of us were tired, grumpy and fed-up but we had at least got 23 miles under our kayaks. We were moving again!

That did not last as the next day was hideous with a Force 7 gusting to Force 8 wind blasting across the whole area. The resultant sea state was both impressive and frightening. The phrase 'Flaming June' took on a whole new meaning, so we pretty much hibernated all day, only emerging to scrounge water from one of the nearby houses.

Progress was resumed on the Wednesday after a night alternating totally calm periods with blasts of wind and rain. By morning the wind was going in our direction, so we once again struggled over the boulders and set off for the Summer Isles in the rain. These are a small group of islands off the entrance to Loch Broom, and are renowned as a kayaking and wildlife-watching destination. Much of the waters around them are shallow, so at the right stage of the tide kayaking amongst them is like gliding over the top of an aquarium pool, looking at all the sea life beneath. The isles themselves were as beautiful as I remembered, and we just made the drying passage behind Isle Ristol before it dried out. We landed on a slab near Rubha Coigeach for lunch, after which I provided Cath with some entertainment by going up the slab to scout the next crossing. Going up was straightforward; coming back down was not and I did the last 20 feet or so in a rush. I was lucky not to end up in the water! We did a long crossing to Clachtoll and then up to the Point of Stoer in driving rain and a following sea which at least gave us a good lift. Slipping round the back of the Old Man of Stoer, a noted sea stack for climbers, we decided to call it a day in Culkein having had a good day after 29 miles. We had also seen eagles, northern divers and skuas, so the bird list was coming on nicely as well. A good day had an even better close when we were allowed in for showers by a nice couple in the caravan near the slip – thank you Simon and Rachel.

Thursday 19 June was 'a day of two halves'. We first enjoyed a lovely sunny morning during which we made good progress on a long series of island hops across Badcall Bay and then around Scourie and into the Sound of Handa. We had hoped to go up the outside, but the wind got up, kicking up quite a sea state, so we stayed 'inside'. Lunch was cold, so we did not linger long, setting off to get around into Kinlochbervie. This small town would be the jumping off point for going around Cape Wrath. Unfortunately, the weather deteriorated at the same time, so just as we committed ourselves to the headland and ensuing crossing, we found ourselves again paddling for our lives. A very unpleasant mile and a half later, we crossed a reef and skated around into the outer approach to Kinlochbervie. The wind remained a pain as it now blasted us from the righthand side, making our final passage into the harbour much harder work than it needed to be. On arrival, wet, cold and bedraggled, we were made extraordinarily welcome. The Harbour Master showed us a sheltered (if not terribly scenic) place to pitch the tents, the Seamen's Mission welcomed us for food, showers and washing, and we found out there was a hotel, phone and Spar supermarket all within easy walking distance. Talking to Kevin, a lobster pot fisherman, we found that the forecast was likely to keep us in the harbour over the weekend; well, there are worse places to get stuck! We had done 18 miles in the day, taking our trip total to 841 miles.

Midges for breakfast in the Sound of Mull.

Beachcomber Cottage, Sand.

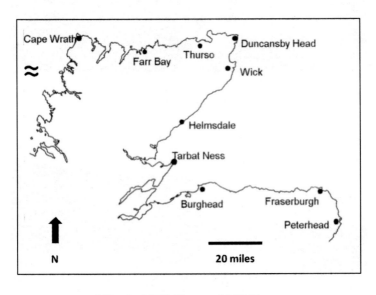

Map 6 – North Coast and NE Corner

North Coast Adventures

It was in fact four days later that we got out of Kinlochbervie. The weather had continued to blow and even the lobster pot men were staying ashore. We left very early, aiming to get around Cape Wrath with the morning tide. Kevin left in his lobster pot boat 15 minutes before us on the dot of 4 a.m. and we were out at 4.15. Progress up to the south side of Sandwood Bay was good and we sneaked a break under the imposing stack of Am Buchaille. Leaving there, I got hit by two large waves, both of which soaked me, and the second of which scared me. I thought I was in for another 'backward loop with loaded boat onto rocks' scenario, but fortunately I again got away with it.

In 1998 I led a group of paddlers on a circumnavigation of the Queen Charlotte Islands of British Columbia. The expedition lasted 6 weeks and had all the good and bad elements of any extended trip. One of the problems for me was that the party size of seven sometimes got in the way of a full enjoyment of the scenery, atmosphere and ambience. As a result, I returned in 2000 with three friends to paddle again the scenic southern island of Moresby. During this trip, whilst exploring the adjacent island of Kunghit, I nearly died. We were crossing a broad shallow area in thick mist when a big swell set came through. They jacked up on the submarine ledges and became towering green monsters. Ann and I turned seaward in our single kayaks, turned on the afterburners and made it clear over the top, getting airborne off the back of each monster wave. Tony and Angelika, paddling a heavily laden double kayak were not so lucky, getting hit hard, leading to them capsizing. When everything calmed down a little, it took some time for Ann and I to spot them. They were in a dangerous position in front of a reef of rocks covered in razor sharp giant shellfish. We effected a very quick rescue and then Ann escorted them to shelter behind the reef whilst I started to pick up all sorts of deck and cockpit cargo that was floating around. Suddenly I realised that the sea level was dropping rapidly; another set was coming in and towering way above me. I did not think I would survive. I was wearing an inflatable lifejacket rather than a buoyancy aid, and no helmet. I had little protection were I to be thrown backwards on to the reef. Ann screamed a warning – which I did not hear – and then I again turned on the afterburners and paddled for my life. I dug holes in the water I was pulling so hard on my paddles. I was lucky in that I hit the top section of the wave just under the crest with sufficient speed in a heavily laden boat to burst through and go airborne. I dropped for what seemed like forever, landing with a shattering crash in the trough. Surviving the next two waves was simple by comparison. Paddling rapidly back around the reef, I rejoined the others. All of us were shocked – and I was lucky to be alive.

Cape Wrath is a major point on any trip on the north west coast, and one of the 'four corners' of a circumnavigation. (The others are Duncansby Head in the north east, North Foreland in the south east and lastly Land's End/Cape Cornwall in the south west. All have their challenges to navigation.) Cape Wrath gets its name from the Old Norse word 'hvarf', 'corner' or 'turning point', as it was as significant to Viking sailors as those of the modern ages. The tides here are somewhat peculiar, running one way for nine hours and then back for three hours – at three times the speed. There was no room here for a cavalier approach to planning and navigation and much of the time in Kinlochbervie had been spent poring over tidal stream atlases and tide tables. Getting our timing right was critical.

Having survived my scare by Am Buchaille, it became apparent that a monster swell was running into Sandwood Bay. This started to raise caution flags with both of us and suddenly turned into a full scale 'red card' when we realised that we were being swept towards the Cape at an extraordinary rate – 'right turn Clyde'! We crashed into a small nook and had a think... I had been around the Cape before, and had vivid memories of being somewhere that I should not have been; I did not need to repeat the experience. Just then, Kevin's lobster pot boat appeared around the corner, rolling heavily in the swell and confused sea. He came out onto the rear deck, stuck his arms out like an airplane and imitated a heavy rolling sea – 'I wouldn't go round there if I were you – it's horrible!' We faced a dilemma: should we return to Kinlochbervie? Although well supplied with 'amenities', four days camped next to the fuel supply tank was probably enough. Or should we try and get ashore? We took the second option, and at last found a small storm cobble beach behind a reef, giving us just enough shelter to get in. By now, of course, the wind had got up again and was creating a huge sea in combination with the swell. Whatever the site was like, it was now 'home'. A small valley with a stream running down provided two flat areas for the tents, and we were soon in. Less welcome was the forecast, which had deteriorated somewhat.

We seemed likely to be here for a few days, which would do nothing good for my state of mind about going round the Cape. Cape Wrath has a justified reputation for committing paddling far from help. If going eastbound, there is only Kearvaig Bay before a long no-landing zone created by the MOD ranges – and Kearvaig can be a non-starter if there is a heavy swell running in.

On several early expeditions to Alaska and western Canada, I experienced what might be euphemistically called 'medical close shaves'. After a fairly nasty incident in which a paddler managed to inflict a serious spiral cut down the whole length of one finger, I decided that I needed more wilderness medical training. As a result I attended the first Wilderness Emergency Medical Technician course to be run in the UK, doing sufficiently well to be subsequently invited to join the Faculty as a probationer. Over time I became a full member of the Faculty, and still teach on the Wilderness Emergency Medical Technician and Wilderness First Responder courses run in the UK and Eire each year. The one disadvantage of being more medically aware is that although I am now better prepared to look after others, who looks after me if I am injured? Although we had so far had no major incidents or accidents, little did I know that in two days time my underlying, and usually controlled, heart condition would erupt, potentially bringing the expedition to an abrupt and premature end.

Two days later the wind dropped and all looked well. We

took a walk to the lighthouse and checked out the view of the far side; all looked good in Kearvaig Bay and beyond. Going back to the tents, we started to pack. I decided that I needed a last look from the top of the nearby hill to calm my nerves and went up it far too quickly. At the top, the view was good, but I had an erratic and forceful heartbeat. I had gone into an episode of atrial fibrillation. Unfortunately the combination of being worked up about the Cape and running up the hill had done for me. I tried resting, both on the hill and back at the tent, and took extra meds but to no effect. Eventually Cath realised that I had stopped doing anything and came across. We had discussed the possible problems before the trip, so it was not unknown to her. After an hour had passed with no change, Cath decided it was her turn to go to the top of the same hill with the radio, and call the Coastguard. 45 minutes later a large Coastguard helicopter came into view. Cath talked to them on the radio and guided them in using one of our smoke flares to give the pilot an idea of the local wind. I had spent the interim writing out a full patient assessment form, using my own medical kit, and rather surprised the paramedic when I gave him the completed form. However, the tables were rapidly turned as I had forgotten to put my name on the top of the form! There had been a second person landed from the helicopter; this turned out to be a cameraman for the Channel 5 series Highland Emergency and we subsequently appeared as the stars of one of the series' episodes. We were flown to Raigmore Hospital in Inverness with just light bags, leaving everything else behind. There was very little chance of anything happening to it out there. The short version of the next 24 hours is 'needles, drugs, sleep, discharge from hospital'. (A little light relief occurred when the A&E doctor and I simultaneously recognised each other from a wilderness medical course he had attended and I had worked on.) I was very relieved to get the all-clear to continue from the consultant cardiologist, having thought for a while that this was the end of the trip for me.

So, there we were in Inverness, with a change of underwear and nowhere to stay!

The youth hostel was fully booked, so a little while later we found ourselves a B&B to stay for two nights. I had spoken to Carol and she would come up to Inverness to take us back to Durness. From there we still had to get back to Cape Wrath. Coming up with Carol would be a friend from Oban, Colin McWilliams. He was a good paddler and had agreed to paddle the north coast with us to give us support in numbers round to Inverness. He thought he would be away from home for about two weeks… He was committed to a job for a few days, so in the interim Cath and I discovered all the delights of Inverness, managing to spend a small fortune in the process. Eventually however, we all met in the supermarket car park and went north. Whilst waiting to come up, Carol had contacted John Orr, the gentleman who now had the lease on the buildings near the Cape Wrath lighthouse and was planning to open a café and bunkhouse. He was ready to take us across from Durness to the Cape road in his boat and then transport us together with Colin's kayak to the top of the slope near the campsite. And after a night in a B&B at Durness, that is what happened.

The three of us were dropped about one (land) mile from

the camp. Fortunately from there it was all downhill across dry-ish bog. This enabled Colin and I to manhaul his kayak whilst Cath carried the last few bits we could not easily get in. I am not at all sure that this was what the cardiologist had in mind when he cleared me to continue the trip..! As we approached the site, it was a relief to see that after nearly six days everything was still there. Colin picked up on the fact that both Cath and I had gone quiet as we arrived and he insisted that we prepared to leave that afternoon rather than wait until the morning, getting wound up again as we did so. He was entirely right, and it was the right thing to do. So, after we had cleared out the rocks from the kayaks (put there to weight the boats down in the wind) and disposed of some spectacular pork pies which were well past their use-by date, we were ready to launch. This in itself was an interesting process. We had arrived at high water on spring tides and were now leaving on neap tides. As a result there was rather less water and a lot more rocks over which to manhandle the boats. A looming black cloud did nothing to encourage my peace of mind and it was with very mixed feelings that I took to the water. As a result, I was keen to get to Kearvaig as fast as possible, so I rather ignored the spectacular scenery and pushed on. Colin went through the arches at the very tip of the Cape, and in retrospect, I wish I had done so too. The landing in Kearvaig was relatively straightforward once we had got around the offshore sandbar with its associated break, and we ended up at the top of the beach with a spectacular view of the sunset.

It had taken Cath and I six days to progress three miles, but at least we were around Cape Wrath and truly on the north coast. One corner down.

From Kearvaig to Faraid Head, you have to pass the MOD range, which includes the offshore island Garbh an Eilean, on which the erosion caused by shellfire and bomb strikes was obvious and scarring. As we neared Smoo Cave, a collapsed fault line known locally as a geo, Cath suddenly called for help. From the tone of her voice, it was clear that whatever it was, it was serious. Paddling across to her, we found that her eyesight had 'gone funny'. She described it as though she was looking at a broken mirror still in its frame – the picture she was seeing was still there, but distorted and fractured. It gradually returned to normal as we shepherded her into the Smoo inlet, but it had evidently been a rather frightening experience. After landing at the back of the inlet, we rested. I went into full 'wilderness medic' mode, carrying out a neurological assessment of Cath – testing responses, reflexes and sensation. Nothing untoward was obvious, and we put the episode down to some form of stress response by her body. Fortunately it never recurred and joined our list of the minor, and sometimes bizarre, ailments which can affect people on long trips.

A rest and something to eat put us all back on the road across to Whiten Head and the spectacular caves and arches. At this point we lost the plot. In an attempt to win back some lost miles and time, we pushed on east of the Rabbit Islands and Eilean nan Ron into Farr Bay. We were all by turns withdrawn and grumpy and even the spectacular arches and tunnels failed to completely lift us. We camped at the top of the beach late into the evening after 25 miles. My diary recorded:

'Far too long a day. Tired. Grumpy. Now 2217 hrs and still not sorted. Bloody ridiculous.'

Two days later we were told that only the previous day the whole bay had been full of dolphins and porpoises hanging quietly in the water, hiding from a transient pod of orca heading up to the Orkney Isles.

The plan was to get around Strathy Point, missing out Armadale Bay. Armadale held bad memories for me as it was there I had had one of my more spectacular surf landings years ago, and I felt no urge whatsoever to repeat the experience. Coincidentally three people I knew, Harry Whelan, Barry Shaw and Phil Clegg whilst on their circumnavigation a couple of years earlier, had an absolute epic getting ashore there with pitchpoled boats, swimmers, a dislocated shoulder and lost gear. The forecast was not great, but the local weather looked passable, so off we went. For a while, all went well. Getting around the points was straightforward, apart from Cath giving me a serious fright by opting to run right across a boomer patch, but it became increasingly tiresome making headway across the bays into a rising Force 5 wind. So Plan A became Plan B – into Armadale Bay. Sheltering from the easterly wind, we camped right at the top of the beach in the corner, where there was just room for the three tents. We still hoped to be in Thurso the following day, and left a phone message to that effect with Ken Nicol, a local paddler and all-round good chap, who had agreed to help us out on this stretch of the journey.

Actually we spent the next three days stuck in the bay as a Force 8 gale sprang up, moving around to the north and sending in big surf. We had to move the tents to a river entrance at the middle of the bay. We did this not a moment too soon as the next high tide sent waves sweeping over our original campsite. Footprints in the sand revealed the presence of otters, but we never saw any. Cath and I narrowly avoided a tent fire when a stove went walkabout during dinner. This was not a good experience and rather reinforced my feelings about the bay. It is fortunate that Bettyhill, a nearby village, has both a café and village store; sitting still on expeditions plays havoc with the planning for meals and food resupply. The evening before we finally moved again, Colin had an amusing encounter… Feeling the need for a visit to the loo at nearly midnight, he scrambled from his tent dressed only in his tee shirt. Having 'done the business', he stood and admired the clearing sky and improving sea state. Getting the feeling that he was being watched, he turned around (remember, he is not wearing a lot) to see the somewhat perplexed couple who had come down to the beach for a quiet time and who were standing 20 metres away on the far side of the river. The sound of the water running over the stones had completely masked their approach. Being a true gentleman, Colin wished them 'goodnight' and retired smartly to his tent!

Getting out through the surf the next day reminded me to put up my hood before taking waves over the head, rather than just afterwards, as the surf lines die away. A damp start for all of us. The coast along to the site of the nuclear power station at Dounreay was interesting, albeit a cold journey in the wind. We took lunch at Sandside Bay, only belatedly realising that this is where several radioactive particles from Dounreay have been found. Not the place for sandcastles, and we were diligent about washing the sand off our feet whilst re-embarking.

The nuclear plant at Dounreay is in the process of being decommissioned, but an ongoing problem is the discovery of radioactive particles on many of the local beaches. The particles, known colloquially as 'hotspots', are linked to the reprocessing of nuclear fuel rods at Dounreay during the 1960's and 1970's, when they were flushed into the sea through the plant's liquid discharge pipe. Interestingly, as we had passed Sellafield on the west coast of the Lake District we saw a strangely shaped vehicle slowly traversing the sands at low tide. It was searching for radioactive particles.

The afternoon was stressful for me, and I do not really know why. We had to go out a long way to avoid the reef off Brims Ness, and I was very glad to pull in to Scrabster. Matters were not improved by eating a piece of chocolate. The first bite broke a filling, and that really got my attention. Not only were we looking for a place to camp, I was now in dire need of a dentist. Ken Nicol came to our rescue and within the space of an hour he had not only arranged for us to have the run of the Pentland Firth Sailing Club, but arranged a dental appointment for me for the following day. On the down side, his opinion was that we would be here for a few days. The forecast had deteriorated yet again, probably pinning us at Scrabster until the weekend.

For three days we enjoyed the hospitality of the Sailing Club, the meals at the Seamen's Mission and the delights of Thurso – even the dentist. The forecast for Sunday looked promising, and on Saturday Cath and I became a stand at the Scrabster Lifeboat Day, collecting money from people who came and talked to us about our journey. It was humbling to realise that those who gave the most were the crews of the lifeboats from either side; the sense of being amongst a 'lifeboat family' was very strong.

Sitting now at the top of Britain, it seemed fitting that a discussion over dinner that night revolved around what constituted 'a circumnavigation'. My view, rightly or wrongly, was that it had to consist of a continuous journey with breaks only being imposed by weather or short-term illness. By that definition, a successful circumnavigation for us was looking unlikely. We were going to run out of time if we continued to be hit by headwinds and bad weather. That did not mean we had to stop our expedition there and then, but we certainly started to think through some of the consequences. Not the least of these was what to name a voyage or voyages that 'go all the way round, but not in one go'? Does a series of day trips covering the whole coastline count as a circumnavigation? Talk as we did, we never came to an answer to that question!

The Coastguard arrives at Cape Wrath!

RNLI Day at Scrabster.

John O'Groats

A Hidden Gem:
Scotland's North East Corner

Philosophy was left behind the following morning as we left our hosts waving good bye, and headed across to Dunnet Head, the most northerly point of the British mainland. We enjoyed spectacular views of both the cliffs above us and the coastline of Orkney, amidst clouds of puffins on the water. We had timed our run to make sure we got through the tide race of the Merry Men of Mey without difficulty, aiming for somewhere around John O'Groats. We got a little ahead of ourselves, leaving enough time for Cath and I to do the tourist bit of having our photo taken at the signpost at John O'Groats before heading to the far northeast tip of the mainland, Duncansby Head. We had been warned of what to expect by Ken: fast tides and stunning scenery, and he was right on both accounts. The headland was riddled with caves, gullies and arches, and the world famous rock stacks around the corner were even better. It was a well pleased trio that eventually pulled in to Freswick Bay late in the evening after an enjoyable 24 miles. Two corners down.

Three months on the trip! Just to celebrate, a beam wind crossing the bays gave an indication of the delightful headwind awaiting us as the coastline swung to the southwest. We fought the Force 6 for a bit, sneaking around the points and sticking close to the back of the coves, but eventually called it a day at

Whaligoe Steps, where a man on the cliffs shouted 'come on up, I've just cut the grass for you!'. Rather suspecting that he was 'taking the piss', we landed, only to find that he had just done exactly that! Davy was the self-appointed guardian of the Steps and landing, and told us much about the history of the place. His grandfather was one of the last people to make a living from landing catches at the steps, and his female forebears then had the unenviable task of taking the catch to the cliff top for transport to market. It had been a good day, and we sat on the grass after dinner, out of the wind and watching an eagle search the cliff line opposite.

Unfortunately the wind continued to blow mightily for the next two days, so we had ample time to explore the delights of Wick. Davy looked after us, providing water, charging our batteries and on the last evening bringing us bottles of beer.

Running south, after a pleasant send off, we passed wonderful scenery and the little villages of Lybster, Berriedale and Helmsdale. This section of coastline is one of the undeclared secrets of the paddling world. It is wonderfully rewarding, providing you are prepared to take on the committing coastline. The weather came in towards the end of the afternoon, so we were a bit wet as we made ourselves comfortable on the shore next to Brora golf course – another developing theme of our campsites. We were well pleased to have made 31 miles after losing two, admittedly pleasant, days in Whaligoe.

The crossing to Tarbet Ness saw us keeping a long way out to avoid the bombing range at Tain which was in operation. RAF Tornados on low level bombing runs are very noisy! The crossing was straightforward, if not terribly inspiring. Colin found his top gear and disappeared ahead whilst Cath and I continued with our 'expedition plod' speed. Meeting up again under the lighthouse, we decided not to cross directly to Burghead, but to go in towards Hilton of Cadboll and take the shorter crossing from there. Halfway through the afternoon, the sea calmed right down, but we were feeling the effects of the long previous day, so decided to stick with the amended plan. The campsite was nice, sheltered as it was under a field wall, but it was disappointing to discover that the pub was shut – on a Friday in Scotland! Cath had an upset with her cooking water which led to her standing in the sea for 10 minutes to cool her feet down whilst saying 'ouch' or something like that. We were lucky to get away that lightly; burns and scalds are common, and dangerous, expedition injuries. My, rather more minor, disaster was to discover that the travel wash container had come open in my admin bag. Fortunately it was not the one with my wallet in it! Cleaning up took rather a long time and was, as I recorded in my diary, tedious. And the weather forecast deteriorated again. Where had summer gone? Awaking to a wind howling over us, it became quickly apparent that we were going nowhere that day; Colin contacted his partner Gill and arranged to be picked up that evening. His leave pass was well overdue with all the days lost to weather since Cape Wrath, but we were very grateful to have had his support and company along the north coast and down around the north east corner. The smiles on both their faces as we all met at 8 o'clock that evening said it all.

So then Cath and I were back to being 'just us'. It felt a little strange as we walked around the village the following morning, still beached by the wind. Looking at the trip log, we discovered that we had done 1001 miles since Ilfracombe, so a celebratory cake or two was enjoyed to mark the occasion. It was also apparent that we were back in the land of 'people' with almost the entire shoreline dotted with cottages and houses as far as the eye could see. Manmade objects were intruding into the natural landscape and this was a marked change from what we had experienced almost since entering Scotland on the west coast many weeks earlier. In retrospect, this change also marked a turning point in our approach to the expedition. Never again would we both walk away from our boats and tents with no fear of anything untoward happening to them. From here on in, outside of 'proper campsites', one of us would always remain with our kit at all times.

The crossing to Burghead started well, but halfway across it became horribly apparent that a huge swell was running in from the east, then wrapping southwards. This gave us real concern about our landing. Because of this, we altered course to go well inland and then followed the coast east towards Burghead. Even from three miles off, we could see waves breaking thunderously over the harbour walls, with walls of water sweeping around the end to go crashing onto the beach. Life got even more tense when we spotted that we were being swept out beyond the harbour by a monstrous back eddy, heading towards an area of water that was thoroughly uninviting. We pulled very hard to get in to the harbour in one piece. We had clearly been watched. As our boats grounded at the back of the harbour, a Coastguard came down for a chat. He was pleased to discover that we had no intention of going further that day; the swell would close out every harbour

Burghead - looking back north.

entrance for the next 20 miles (and we were not entertaining the thought of a beach surf landing in those conditions). My diary records:

'Walked up to the head and looked along the coast – YE GODS! The last time I saw surf like that was on the Atlantic coast of the Gironde in France. Absolutely no question of going any further today.'

There is a proper campsite just west of Burghead, so we launched back into the harbour and scuttled across to it. We got booked in for the night and used the showers and laundry; it was hard to know which was more welcome. It was a nice day, bar the horrendous wind and gigantic swell, and it felt acceptable to be stopped for plainly obvious reasons rather than anything which could be interpreted by others as lack of moral fibre. We had decided right from the start of the planning for the expedition that it was to be 'our' trip and that we were not beholden to anyone else. Nonetheless a creeping feeling that, for me at least, our trip had to stand scrutiny from my paddling peers had established itself in my head. Such is the psychology of expeditions!

Tuesday 22 July – Day 100. Low water on spring tides meant a very long way to the water's edge, so we made two rather long trolley runs to get the boats to the harbour and the water. In the process, we recorded our latest start yet at 1145. Thereafter it was a good run along the cliffs to Hopeman and Lossiemouth. Here Cath had two aquatic moments, falling in both on getting out for lunch and then on getting back in again. She was furious about getting soaked twice, so it was a bit quiet heading out across the long expanse of Spey Bay. The back of the bay was an extraordinary backdrop with a long gravel beach topped with conifers. It looked more like Alaska than anything we had expected for Scotland. The Spey was in spate after all the rain, so from half way onwards, the sea was thick with peat and uprooted trees. Buckie did nothing to attract us to stay, so we pressed on a little further to Findochty where we found a small east facing cove which became home for the night. Here we met with Lester Matthews (a.k.a. 'Lester the Jester'). He was on his way home after a Duke of Edinburgh award expedition down the Spey, and decided to join us for a couple of days. It was a lovely calm evening, with the promise of two days of good weather to follow. It was indeed Day 100, but by this stage we had already had 42 non-paddling days; it seemed certain that 2008 was not destined to be a vintage sea kayak expedition year.

We were accompanied by dolphins as we moved along to Banff, smelling their breath as much as seeing and hearing them. Lunch at Banff was enlivened by a sporty surf landing (three boats on the same wave has possibilities for all sorts of aquatic carnage), and then the customary afternoon headwind kicked in. As a result of this, we only clawed our way to Macduff before admitting defeat. We were not pleased, but it was very hard work against the wind. Two local boys, Andrew and Bradley, befriended us, giving us two postcards to wish us well with our journey. Sometimes it is the small gestures of friendship and support that really hit home; I wish I had not been so preoccupied with the daily planning routine whilst they were with us. Eventually the nightlife of Macduff quietened down but then the gulls started, so a good night's sleep was not enjoyed by any of us. Lester also suffered mightily from the midges in the grass patch he was camped on. He had obviously been too long on the Spey, camping under his upturned open boat. His tent was an open-sided tarp, which clearly meant midge heaven. As a result, we got away with some speed and into another wonderful section of the coast. Troup Head has a huge gannetry, with both the sea and sky full of birds. Arriving at Rosehearty, we were stopped again by headwinds; the next section to Fraserburgh is open and flat, and that gave us no chance of sneaking in under the lee of the coast. The campsite was both official and part-time; we had to call the owners to let them know we were there and would like a key for the shower and toilet block. The forecast was again unfavourable – something we were gradually becoming resigned to – so Lester decided that two days was enough and started a very complicated operation to get back to his car at Findochty. Only 30 miles away by sea, he had to take two buses to get there, the first one going in the wrong direction. He reappeared late in the evening, very grateful to discover that Cath and I had found and put up his very complicated micro-tent. It was more of a nylon coffin or body bag than anything I would want to use.

The wind was indeed 'up' the following morning, so Lester left us to continue his journey home. Before he left, he said a prayer for us. This was simultaneously both reassuring and uncomfortable as neither Cath nor I are particularly religious. Cath and I walked to the shop, discovering that rather than paved with gold, most of the streets of Rosehearty were paved with dog excrement. It was exceedingly unpleasant. The shop was expensive too. The rest of the day was spent in an orgy of washing clothes and bodies and doing all sorts of administration. All the boat bits that needed fixing were, and when we ran out of jobs, we retired to bed, hoping that the local youths were not going to be as noisy as the night before.

They were quiet, so we slept well. The sun came up, and the wind dropped to a mild head breeze, so off we went to Fraserburgh. Fraserburgh was psychologically important to us as it was the half way point of the planned trip. We had, however, taken 104 days to get there. There was a sad looking fishing vessel, the Sovereign, wrecked on a reef just east of the town. Passing the section of coast to Peterhead via Rattray Head was a rather long and cold process, along never ending sand dunes. Sand dunes are, in my opinion, an acquired taste when paddling along them. It is difficult to judge progress and they are, inevitably, repetitious to look at. We came to the conclusion that camels ought to be an indigenous species in Scotland! Peterhead power station outflow warmed the bay nicely, even to the extent that I paddled right up to a seal sleeping in the warm water. It was far too comfortable to be worried about a pair of kayaks. Thereafter we had a nice late afternoon run down past the cliffs to Port Errol at the northern end of Cruden Bay. There was a significant swell running in, so we kept a little way off. Even so, it was either 'technical' or 'yee hah!' depending on your preference.

We raced the thick North Sea mist known locally as the haar into Port Errol; the clammy atmosphere rather encouraged us to get the tents up quickly. A lady in one of the houses came out to offer us hot chocolate; an offer that was gladly accepted. The weather was still 'claggy' the following morning, so we gratefully took an hour lie in. Then it cleared so we packed. We had almost finished and then the rain and mist came back with a vengeance. We retired to Cath's tent and had a think. She went to the phone box and I contemplated the next section of cliffs down to the top of the bay north of Aberdeen. This was a somewhat scary prospect given swell and poor visibility. My musings were interrupted by the lady of the house opposite again; I was abducted and force-fed tea and pancakes! Cath tracked me down a short while later, so we chatted with the couple in the house, keeping an eye on the weather. Just before our credibility ran out, the weather let up, so we finished packing and set off. Inevitably, given the way these things go, we had just cleared Cruden Bay when the visibility went, and this time totally. This resulted in a very scary two hours of finger tip navigation down towards Aberdeen. At the start of the dunes, still some 10 miles north of Aberdeen, the swell really picked up and we made a half-hearted and probably inadvisable attempt to land on a shore we could not see and did not know. A big swell set came through, nearly picking us up and certainly scaring the pair of us. Much as I hated to do so, we back-tracked up the cliffs in thick fog to find the entrance to the small harbour of Collieston. We managed to find it, but even with GPS on, it was still really hard to spot the slot leading into the harbour. We then had to time our approach to avoid getting wiped out on the rocks to the south of the entrance. I think we both aged a little during that process. The only place to camp was on a small strip of grass in front of the public toilets, with a dog poo bin between the tents… Beggars can't be choosers.

Neither of us had enjoyed the day, and Cath in particular found it very hard and scary. We had paddled 10 miles, but only made six forward; whatever else, we would not be moving until we could see what was going on. We had had enough of cliffs, swell and surf in zero visibility. We had a long conversation about going on or stopping, without coming to a clear conclusion. Everyone has a 'down' patch somewhere on a long trip, and this was Cath's. She almost seemed to want me to tell her to stop, but I had always said that that was a decision that we each had to take for ourselves. In purely selfish terms, I knew that if she left I would have a hard time continuing alone; the logistics of getting a boat to and from the water each day unaided is a major challenge. On the other hand, I could not force her to stay – but I certainly hoped she would. I was probably horribly unsympathetic to her dilemma, and then insufficiently appreciative when she decided to carry on. I still give myself a hard time over that.

We remained stuck at Collieston for the next two days; no visibility, rain and a huge swell kept us firmly ashore. Collieston is a nice village, albeit somewhat 'weird'. Some people were very welcoming and supportive, some rather less so. A local pastime appears to be nude pier jumping, accompanied by shouts of glee, at dark o'clock… Cath's boyfriend Trevor came and found us, so we all went to Aberdeen on the second day, enjoying the delights of the granite city. As when Carol came across to us in South Wales, I think that Cath enjoyed the respite from me but did not enjoy the inevitable farewell that accompanies any visit. On the Wednesday, the visibility allowed us to make a tentative start as the sun was forecast to break through the mist late morning. I nearly had a more exciting start than I wanted. A large wave nibbled at me as I left the harbour, nearly resulting in an unplanned aquatic moment. We got to our previous turn back point in good order, but not entirely pleased that we still could not see very much. Staying out, we navigated by ear until opposite the river entrance at Newborough, half way along the dunes. We fancied a beach break from the stress! Then, typically, all visibility went again, and big swells came rolling in. I was forcibly picked up by one and sent shoreward. Cath fought the next one, in the process entirely losing sight of me. When I grounded – it had been an exciting ride in – I did not know whether I was on a sandbank or the shore, and I had no idea where Cath was. My primary concern was that she was upright and still OK. I stood, wondering what to do – was she left or right of me? All of a sudden the mist cleared and we had limitless visibility. Cath was about 100 metres south of me – having the same thoughts about where on the beach I was. It was good to get back together. We had a long break on the beach and then it was off on another 'sand dune afternoon' to Aberdeen.

By now we had become very aware that the nature and character of the east coast was markedly different to that of the west. The seas seemed to be shorter and sharper in shape and manner and the beaches were either long flat affairs or steep shingle ones. The scenery was different too, with cliff lines being generally lower and often of softer rock. When combined with the greater presence of people and industry, the east felt like the poor relation compared to some of the vistas and grandeur of the west.

We knew from the quick visit that we had made the day before that camping possibilities were going to be limited, so we decided to try our luck at the mouth of the River Don. This was nearly our undoing, as at the worst possible moment the swell jacked up and we found ourselves right in the middle of the fun zone – except that it was not fun at all. We aborted that plan and headed across to Aberdeen harbour entrance. We could just see a tiny beach inside the outer breakwater arm and we thought it would give us a swell free landing. The site itself was not wonderful (city camps usually are sub-optimal), but we had a grandstand view of the harbour entrance. As if to welcome us, we then sat and watched a two hour matinee performance given by a school of dolphins. There must have been at least 30 of them, and there were usually three or four in the air all the time; it was a wonderful show in the sun and wind. A little later on, Trevor found us, in the process earning many plus points by bringing a barbecue and cooking dinner. A slight downside to the location was that all Scotland's spiders seemed to live in the long grass there. Cath 'doesn't do' spiders…

We stayed at the harbour entrance for another two days; a huge swell with seas breaking over the harbour breakwater did nothing to entice us out. Nor did the knowledge that all the small harbours on the next stretch of coast south face directly into where the swell was running. This meant that we effectively faced a 40 mile no-landing zone in those conditions. The dolphins were good on the first day, but if they were there on the second, we could not see them. Actually, we could not see across the harbour entrance as the fog was clamped in very hard. The routine of 'paddle one day, get stuck for two days' was beginning to become somewhat trying; we desperately wanted to get on and make progress. In the afternoon, Trevor left for the mountains on the west coast, and we were joined by a friend of mine, Jim Savege, who had stolen a long weekend pass and come to play. The forecast for Saturday 2 August actually looked quite good.

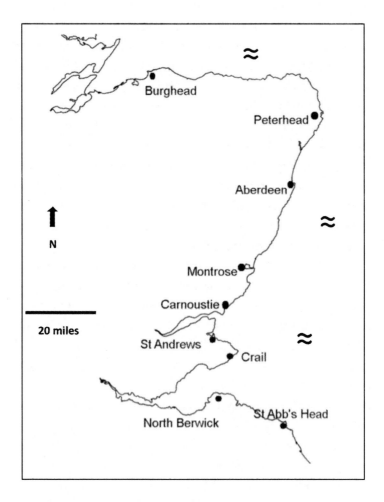

Map 7 – East Coast Scotland

Eastern Scotland

The forecast looked good and so did the actual weather – right up to the point where we were committed to the outside of the point beyond the breakwater. Then we realised the extent of our mistake. The swell was still running hard and big, but at a slightly different direction than before, which was why we thought it had dropped. As well as knowing that all the harbours and landings would still be out, Jim was having a hard time in his kayak. It was of a design more suited to racing in flatter conditions than we were experiencing so he was more concentrated on staying upright than making forward progress. Going back to our campsite was unappealing, but only marginally less so than the surf landing onto rocks that we then did. We had covered the grand total of one nautical mile. Not a good day. Having set up the tents again, in late afternoon the weather gradually improved, so we hoped that we might actually get somewhere the following day. We did, all the way down the Angus coast to Lunan Bay. We had lunch at Catterline in the back of a small harbour and then there was a stretch of superb cliffs taking us to Montrose Bay. This became a bit of a trial in hot sunshine, even after we had awarded ourselves ice creams in Johnstown. In Lunan, we were met by Carol, Ginny and Niamh the dog, who nearly got run down in the surf, so keen was she to come out and say hello. We had a good dinner courtesy of Carol bringing it with her and a resupply of all sorts of goodies. We also changed over all our charts and maps, this being one of the predetermined switch points. 33 miles was a good run, and we were pleased. Our aim was to get at least to St Andrews on the Fife coast next day, but that depended on the weather continuing to behave for a bit.

As we had experienced in South Wales at the very start and then again on parts of the west coast, the thing about big sandy bays is that when the tide goes out, it goes out a very long way. In this respect Lunan Bay was no different to any other and we had another long trolley to get the boats to the water. Paddling along the cliffs to Arbroath was really pleasant in the sunshine, and brought back memories of similar adventures and escapades whilst stationed with 45 Commando Group in Arbroath many years earlier. We had lunch on the golf course at Carnoustie, then a long hot crossing to the Fife coast. We kept well out from the beach at Tentsmuir because the sandbanks there go out a very long way and that was a complication we did not need. It was a long afternoon going to St Andrews and then on to near the tip of Fife. We landed at Cambo Sands and found a good place for the tents. Unfortunately we did not realise that the place was also a favourite with large red, biting ants until after we had all been bitten. Oh well! Having said that, the bites took a long time to heal, and left noticeable scars. Carol and Ginny had met us again and whisked Jim off to Dundee railway station so he could recover his car from Aberdeen. He got back to Cambo long after Cath and I had turned in.

We were up early in the sunshine, getting afloat by 8 a.m.

I managed to leave my tent pegs in the long grass, but fortunately Jim found them before he left, and I was reunited with them a few days later. We had hoped to cross to the Isle of May straightaway, but the tide was still kicking up some nasty overfalls, so we went along to the little fishing village of Crail instead. After a lunch break, allowing the tide to die down, we crossed to the Isle of May then went for the Bass Rock. The forecast had bad weather coming in later, and ideally we wanted to be on the south side of the Firth of Forth, not stuck on the north, lee, shore. In forecast terminology 'later' means after at least 12 hours, normally a long enough bracket to make a crossing and get set up in camp. The weather does not always listen to the forecast and in this instance 'later' turned out to be 'earlier'. We had a long, violent ride towards the Bass, getting swept past in some big seas and dodging a gigantic trawler before landing, soaked, about a mile east of North Berwick. Yet another golf course edge campsite. It was clearly a favourite, with fire rings, rubbish and broken glass in abundance. The view was spectacular though. All in all, it had been a good day with nearly 20 miles done, and a major crossing under our belts. The only down side was that both our sets of paddling gear seemed finally to have given up the ghost. Everything leaked badly, and we were permanently wet and cold. Cath, whose nickname could justifiably be 'Icicle', was especially feeling it. I had a long telephone conversation with Dave Felton at Knoydart, who had been our initial contact with Kokatat, and he had a stunning success. Kokatat decided that we were to be given a new drysuit each, and they would probably arrive in a few days time. Dave was even prepared to drive out and find us to do the swap. Kokatat wanted the suits back to see what had happened to them. It transpired that we had plain worn them out, putting, in Kokatat's opinion, five years of use on them.

Over the next two days, we got to know the beach intimately. A Force 6 wind blew at us constantly, bringing with it driving rain. On the radio we heard reports of major flooding, and much water damage all over east Scotland. Walking into North Berwick was a damp experience and we did not even manage to dry out in the café despite leaving ominously large puddles. On the second day we went up the cliff to a caravan site, where we were allowed to use the showers and laundry. The previous day's efforts at drying thermal underwear by wearing it and sitting in the sleeping bags had been rather unsuccessful. And smelly – although wool remains 'warm when wet' and does not attract the body odour some manmade fabrics do, the odour of 'soggy sheep' filled the tent and competed with the miasma around my socks for unpleasantness. Visitors to the tent do not stay for long at such times. Although Friday dawned bright and sunny, we had a disappointing day, only getting as far as Dunbar because of the sea state kicked up by the previous two days of wind. Just getting ashore at Dunbar was over-exciting with lots of reef breaks and boomers. We managed to miss the harbour entrance itself, a narrow cut in the sandstone cliffs, so we actually arrived on foot and trolley from the east beach. Camping places are somewhat limited in Dunbar but we got onto Lammer Island, next to the ruins of the old military hospital, and cleared enough broken glass to get the tents up. Access to the island is, because of its early history, by a two-section drawbridge. The Harbour Master said he would raise this in the evening, to make sure we were not disturbed by the local 'wildlife'. Because it had been a short day, we got another shopping trip in, did boat maintenance, and whiled away the afternoon, looking at the sky, willing the weather forecast to improve. It did not, so we stayed another day. Dave came with the drysuits and my errant tent pegs and found us in the evening, as did some 'friends of friends' who brought some delicious chocolate cake which was very much appreciated. We noticed that the drawbridge remained down that night; perhaps it was a none too subtle hint that we did not have unlimited time on Lammer Island. Despite this we were not disturbed even when the local Police came to talk to some youngsters on the island. The kids were better at quickly hiding their booze than the Police were at finding it!

Sunday was not good initially; the wind still howled, and the rain still fell, so we had a slow start. Two hours later, things had improved a lot, so we ran before the wind, and with the tide, passing Pease Bay and Cove where a lot of the hillside had collapsed into the sea, a victim of the storms. From Pease southwards, we had a superb afternoon paddle with cliffs all the way to St Abbs. There were many cliff top waterfalls as everywhere was still sodden. St Abbs Head itself was a sea paddling gem with many stacks and caves. There were lots of dive charter boats out and about as well, so we were chatting quite a lot. Beyond St Abbs lay Eyemouth, which we rapidly renamed Eyesore. The beach hit a new high, or probably low, point in the amount of 'poo' we had to move to get the tents up, and walking the beach was a positive minefield experience. We were determined to move the next day, hopefully reaching and crossing the border back into England.

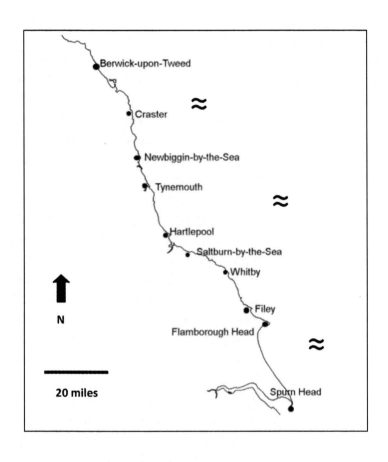

Map 8 – The North East Coast of England

The North East Coast of England

The coast south to the border was mainly sandstone cliffs, leading us to the crossing of the Tweed and England. The actual border is a slightly insignificant beach a bit further north. The river was running hard and dirty as many trees and bushes were coming out of the uplands with the water. I enlivened the relaunch after lunch by completely messing up getting into the boat. I stayed dry thanks to the new drysuit, but the boat flooded totally and was a handful in the beach break as we wrestled with it. It was a long afternoon down to Holy Island, then Bamburgh Castle, where an arctic skua fought a spectacular aerial battle with two terns for their food. As with Blackpool Tower earlier in the trip, Bamburgh Castle can be seen from many miles away and seemed to take an age to reach. We passed inshore of the Farne Islands, heading into Seahouses harbour in search of a landing but in view of the state of the area we came back out quickly. We continued for another mile or so, ending on the beach south of the river. It was a glorious evening, and sufficiently far out of town that there was no danger of disturbance. I celebrated by repairing the hole in the boat hull I had incurred when watching seals at Holy Island, rather than concentrating on the reef I was near. Another good day and at last we seemed to be making progress again.

The 'Glorious 12th' dawned with not a grouse in sight. We paddled south in pouring rain against a backdrop of low cliffs and fields running into the sea – not the sort of thing needed to inspire and spur on a sea paddler. After Dunstanburgh Castle – and a small tussle with a race off the point – we stopped in Craster to refill our water bags. It was upsetting to discover several large crabs without legs and claws at the edge of the sea – it seemed that after the edible parts had been torn off, the bodies were just discarded, presumably still alive. Getting back to the boats, we became aware of a couple taking a lot of interest in our preparations. Just as we went to leave, they introduced themselves as Buddhists, and asked if we would mind if they chanted for us when they got home. After assuring them that we would take any assistance from whatever source, we left the harbour, barely being able to control our smiles. My diary then records that 'it all got grotty – scruffy sand dunes, urban, power station etc etc'. There were also a lot of underwater shelves sticking out a long way, and we had to give them a very wide berth with the swell still running. Sometimes we thought we would need our passports in Norway, we had to go out so far. We pulled in late in the afternoon to Newbiggin-by-the-Sea, paddling around the artificial reef topped by two bizarre statues. The gravel beach had been manicured to within an inch of its life; unfortunately we had to pull two boats 'cross grain' to get to the top of the beach. We certainly left our mark! There was nowhere to go, so we set up camp on the promenade, under the watchful gaze of first a woman on the upper promenade, then a couple of people. I could see this going wrong, probably into the realm of 'you can't camp here', but then everyone disappeared.

About 30 minutes later, two teenagers walked down the promenade towards us, carrying a bottle of wine. Somewhat exasperatedly, I was tired, I muttered under my breath words to the equivalent of 'why could they not go somewhere else and get pissed?' As they got close, one of them asked 'are you

Rowland?' This got the startled response 'it depends who's asking and why!' It transpired that Craig and his mate had recently been on an open boat canoeing course in Scotland with Claire Knifton and Tom Thomas (both friends of mine), and had been told about our adventure. They then followed us on the website, and it was Craig's mum who had been watching us come in and get set up. The wine did not last long. They went and got us fish and chips, took our washing up to Craig's mum's house for a laundry, and took away all the batteries for charging. On top of all that, Cath was whisked away for a bath in the morning, whilst I fended off the local council and took down the tents. Which all goes to show that first impressions of places and people can be somewhat misleading.

We had a slow start as Cath's bath turned into 'breakfast (huge) and bath'. The day was uninspiring 'a right grotty   day – rain, clag, grim scenery, lumpy water… the only good things were getting a tailwind, and a good stream in the afternoon.' We only got off the water to have lunch at Cullercoats; otherwise, we paddled on all day. The streams off Sunderland harbour and again getting into Seaham harbour were fast, creating wild seas and lumpy conditions. As we landed, we dodged the swells breaking clear over the harbour breakwater. Seaham has a history of tragedy when vessels attempt to enter the tiny harbour in bad conditions. Perhaps the most poignant occurred on the 17th of November 1962. The five man crew of the Seaham lifeboat, the George Elmy, and four of the five men they had just rescued, were lost at the entrance to the harbour in gigantic and confused seas kicked up by the swell running in from the North Sea. The story remains alive in the community, with the new coast road being named George Elmy Lifeboat Way in memory of the lives lost. Fortunately we did not learn of that story before we entered; we just thought the swell was a bit aggressive. We set up camp on the concrete, the weather eased a little, and we fielded lots of questions from the locals, who plainly thought we were both mad. Cath, with extensive experience of working with disadvantaged youth, did notice that many of those who came and talked to us had the pinpoint pupils which betray opiate misuse. The swell was due to drop next afternoon and the wind to run NE, creating an onshore breeze from our left rear.

Well, the swell did drop, and the wind did swing to onshore, so we got on just before lunch, getting immediately picked up by the south-going stream. And then it all went badly wrong. We were committed. With the stream running at four knots, we were not going to be able to get back up to Seaham, even if we wanted to. The swell, having dropped right off, came back with a vengeance, and the wind swung around to the west, offshore, and increased to Force 5. We were between the devil and the deep blue sea. The swell was kicking up an enormous surf break which made a beach landing uninviting, but we could not go out to get south of Hartlepool and into the marina, because we would never have got back in against the wind. Stress levels peaked, and all we wanted to do was get off the water. Much against our will, we committed to a surf landing on Hartlepool north beach, next to the ruins of a pier. Local youths fishing off the pier added to our contemplative pleasure by hurling abuse at us – why? With nowhere else to go, we endured one of the scariest surf landings either of us had ever done. Obeying the rule 'do not look back', I did not – until I did, immediately wishing I had not! Walls of black water enveloped us, and we had a slalom run through the remains of a second pier we did not know was there. Thankfully the boats behaved impeccably and we got in without undue incident. We landed on what looked like the set for the next film in the post-Apocalyptic Mad Max series. A partly demolished factory or works was spilling rubbish and waste onto the beach, and feral gangs roamed the remains.

We were not happy! To compound the sense of insecurity, a passer-by said 'don't leave anything unattended here – they'll have it'. What exactly was meant by 'they' was left unspecified. He also told us of a fish and chip shop nearby: 'go along the rail tracks, under the underpass, and it's right opposite'. That did not sound too bad, so leaving Cath guarding the tents and boats, off I set. It turned into the scariest trip for a fish supper I have ever made. The factory ruins went on forever, the underpass was nearly 100 metres long, was dark and flooded, and the chippie was in a war zone. Never have two fish suppers been carried so fast back to the camp! My paranoia was at such a level that I even set up improvised trip wires with cans around the tents, and tied everything to everything else, so as to get a decent warning if anything started up. We did not sleep well. I was determined that, come what may, we were getting off the beach, and out of Dodge, next day.

The day dawned bright and cheerful, so we ignored the surf and launched. We eventually got beyond the break, but it was hard work with both of us taking heavy hits in the process. On the bright side, we were headed out of Hartlepool. We stayed very wide off the point to avoid the reef breaks then headed to the smelly delights of the refinery and steelworks at Teeside. Fortunately the river entrance is relatively narrow, so crossing the traffic was less of a problem than it might have been. By-passing Redcar, we neared the point south of Saltburn. Something was

Teeside Scenery. (C Tanner)

not right. The swell had again picked up, having moderated somewhat at midday, and we now had wind against tide kicking up a nasty sea on top of the swell. We did not fancy going on as the next bay did not look promising on the map. Retreating three miles to Redcar, inside the reef and therefore giving a sheltered landing, was also an unappealing prospect. So we had to face the surf again and get in at Saltburn. I had a superb run in on one wave from about 500 metres out, all the way to the beach. Cath came in shortly afterwards, having had a less adventurous run and staying pretty dry throughout. Both of us were glad to be ashore but the problem now was where to camp? There was nowhere apparent, so we just picked a patch of grass on the side of the road, between the pub and the old mortuary. The fact that every passing car felt the need to honk their horns at us did not bode well for a good night's sleep and Cath attracted a few unwelcome gestures as well. On the plus side, we had a nice meal in the pub. Months later it became obvious that the card transaction was never going to be processed, so it turned out to be a free meal as well.

There was, however, payback: 'dreadful night's sleep – car noise, drunken idiots, nightmares and, finally, early fishermen!' All in all, it was a good job the weather kept us beached, doing so for another two days. During the afternoon of the first day, having exhausted the delights of Saltburn fairly quickly, we became highly motivated to move the tents. Parking by the side of the road was less than ideal. Somewhat chancing my luck, I asked at a nearby house, a converted mill, if we could possibly camp on the grass next to the house – probably their front lawn. Surprisingly Catherine said 'yes', so we moved camp rather smartly, and spent the remaining days in Saltburn trying to be as inconspicuous as possible. I had a disastrous haircut; I hate to think what 'short' would have produced, given the result of 'a trim, please'… On the plus side, the laundrette coped with all our gear, including sleeping bags, so the pong factor reduced a lot.

Escaping after three days, it was a bit of a relief to see the next bay south. It was obvious that it would not have been a good idea to have gone for it earlier. We would never have got in, given the swell that had been running earlier. In the afternoon, after passing tall mud cliffs into Whitby Bay, we hid in the harbour for a while as a huge squall came through. Life became very wet and blowy for a time. Robin Hood's Bay became our day's destination, but we had a lot of trouble finding anywhere to camp as the sea goes right to the mud cliffs, and they were all collapsing after the heavy rains. Eventually we threw ourselves on the mercy of the YHA at Boggle Hole Youth Hostel. After a few sticky moments we were allowed to camp in the nettle patch – but at least it was 'home' and we bought both dinner and breakfast, so no cooking was required. There are a number of owls in the woods near the hostel…!

To continue a theme that ran throughout the expedition, this was an occasion where people went out of their way to help. Camping was listed on the tariff board at the hostel – but technically not allowed at *this* hostel. There were no spare beds and things were looking bleak until the warden decided that we could be the test team for camping on the hillside. Sadly, a very different approach to our campsite was to come in a few days time.

The coast to Scarborough was pretty but sadly the same cannot be said of the town. We were surprised at how committing was the paddling; the landings are few and far between and much of the base of the cliffs is distinctly unwelcoming as a bale-out option. Going south to Filey Brig, we ran with the stream in our favour and were sheltered from the offshore wind. Rounding the end of the Brig changed all that, and we had a hard pull along into Filey itself. Flamborough Head is a major headland and landmark on the east coast with extensive and very high cliffs on the north side contrasting with lower cliffs and extensive shallows on the south. Because the Head runs almost completely west-east, the wind this day blew along both sides of the peninsula and afforded shelter on neither side. Rounding Flamborough Head in these conditions was not an attractive option so we pulled into Filey, ending the day in the dinghy park of the local sailing club. The slipway up to the park was extremely steep and the following morning it was a precarious approach to the water's edge. It was 10 miles across to and along the Bempton Cliffs, to which we could not get particularly close because of the swell; the caves and boomers were exploding with a vengeance. That did not however stop our appreciation of the scenery and a sky full of wheeling and plunging gannets. We had an ice cream break in North Landing, then rounded the end and went to Bridlington; we passed without stopping. We carried on south, fortunately pushed by the tide, only beaching to take 'thunderstorm breaks' – damp and scary experiences. Eventually we got ashore at Hornsea, camping at the top of the gravel beach. Interestingly, this was the only campsite that neither of us took a picture of, and that was something in retrospect that neither of us could explain. It had been a good day in terms of mileage, 26 miles, but the coast of Yorkshire was rapidly becoming a 'not to be repeated' experience. There would be more of those later.

We had another long day getting down to Spurn Head. The

first 25 miles or so were frankly uninspiring with low mud cliffs, all collapsing into the sea. The upside was that at every beach stop, I could go fossil hunting. This area was where my father had grown up and an activity he had taken part in. In turn he introduced it to me to as a small boy but little did I think then that 50 years later I would be back repeating the experience. I remember pulling shiny, curly ammonites and bullet-like belemnites from the mud cliffs as a child and had some success on this occasion. I did have to be reminded by Cath that fossil hunting was not the principal reason for being here… In heavy rain we squeaked over the bar into the Humber Estuary, pulling up late in the evening to camp at the top of the beach near the permanent RNLI crew station. Also nearby was the VTS tower from where all traffic into and out of the Humber and its major ports was controlled. Looking at the shipping, it was alarming to see just how close and how fast the vessels passed the end of the spit. Talking to the VTS watch officers a little later, they agreed to let us know of a 20 minute gap in the traffic the following morning. This would be sufficient to let us sprint across the north channel to the WW2 anti-aircraft tower in the middle of the estuary. From there we could afford to be a little more leisurely crossing to Lincolnshire as that channel is markedly quieter, and used by smaller vessels.

After a really good night's sleep during which the foxes played undisturbed, I broke camp while Cath was away taking the rubbish to the bins. Suddenly, and forcibly, I was treated to the Yorkshire version of farewell: 'you can't camp here!' The obvious response, 'we're packing up to go' only met with several increasingly irritating repetitions of the same message. The obnoxious individual departed with his final shot 'the warden knows you're here and he's on his way down'. He was, but he was also rather more intelligent and appreciated that with no markings on either the map or chart, and with signs only on the landward approach, not from the sea, it was hard to know of the private bird reserve we were in. We were, after all, right in front of the permanent RNLI station and VTS tower – so we were not adding unduly to bird stress in the area. He readily accepted that we were not able to leave until we got the 'go ahead' from VTS, and if the weather changed suddenly we would be, reluctantly, staying.

So, about an hour late, we got the signal to be ready and then left hurriedly as a bulk carrier decided to moor up in the holding area rather than enter the estuary. A swift crossing to the flak tower in the middle of the estuary was given impetus by the approaching shapes of several outbound vessels from Hull and Immingham. Vessels heading seaward out of the Humber do not travel slowly! Unfortunately we could not let VTS know we were across the first channel as both our VHF radios decided to malfunction at the same time. We pushed on to the Lincolnshire shore and landed on a sandbank where we were able to change radio batteries and talk to Spurn Head VTS. As it turned out, they could see us clearly through their gigantic binoculars and were happy with our progress and safety all the way across. That left two more major crossings to go, the Wash and the Thames. My diary records the afternoon as:

'a purgatory of sand and mud at low tide – enlivened only by the seals and alleviated only by the fact that we were going with the tide.'

We landed at Mablethorpe and had a long, long, long trudge to the edge of the dunes where we camped – not realising then that it would be for two more days. As we set up camp we were accosted by a woman demanding to know where was the exit from the beach to the car park. We could not help, having arrived from the sea, but we did make what seemed to us a sensible suggestion. She set off in the opposite direction, turned around about 200 metres away and then came back by us, heading in the direction of Mablethorpe town. I stood there puzzling over her behaviour until Cath came across and said 'did you see her eyes – fully dilated. She's on speed'. That made sense, but made me rather sad as well.

We sat out two days of wind – it was a Bank Holiday weekend, after all – visited Mablethorpe (once only – no revisit required), watched the buggy kite surfers enjoying the flat sands and collected a large number of cowrie shells from the beach. Cath's sister had at some stage worked in Mablethorpe, so she took lots of pictures for her. We opted for a half-tide start on the third day, giving us a shorter struggle to the water, and some tidal assistance with the fight against the headwind. On the way down to Skegness we both recaptured escaping beach toys and reunited them with their owners. The coast is fairly uninteresting with low dunes interspersed with rundown buildings and then, as you reach Skegness, amusement parks. We stopped just next to a hamlet. This did not have a pub, so giving a promising outlook for a quiet night, and once again set up the tents on the edge of a golf course. Rather disappointingly the weather the following day had not read the forecast and decided to be somewhat adverse, south of west and Force 4, so we stayed. We managed to scrounge a shower at the local caravan site then spent the rest of the day hoping the wind would drop. It did at last, so the prospects of getting across the Wash and on to Norfolk started to look a lot better.

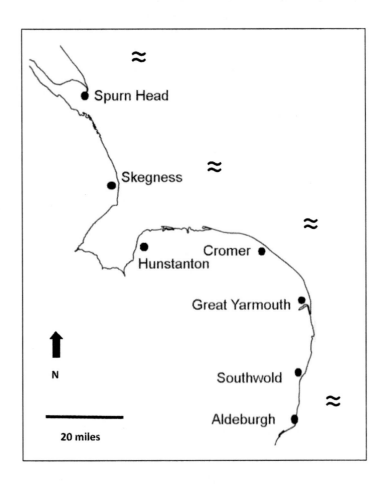

Map 9 – East Anglia

East Anglia

Every so often, everything comes together and the crossing of the Wash was straightforward. With good tidal stream assistance we pushed on and reached Norfolk in under four hours. We did not see much land in the process as everything is low-lying, but some bumps over the sandbanks, arctic skuas, guillemots and a puffin kept us entertained. We opted to land at high water as the drying area goes out a long way. This positioned us just above the tide line, with a short carry to the water for the 6 a.m. start in the morning. Where we were camped gave us a superb sunset, followed all too soon by an equally impressive sunrise. This gave us an atmospheric 'early morning mist' paddle along the north Norfolk coast until the sun really got going, after which we were hot. This was a most unusual sensation! It became a really good day, achieving 26 miles along mostly pretty coastline with sandbanks (not Lincolnshire mud), dunes, beach huts and a forest background. We ran out of steam at West Runton, between Sheringham and Cromer, pulling in to the beach which still had rather a large number of holidaymakers on it. We answered innumerable questions, took donations for the RNLI and finally got the tents up. Then, out of the blue, one person who had been very interested in our trip reappeared carrying fish and chips for two – 'I thought I'd probably delayed your supper too long – so here it is'. He turned out to be Rob Hastings, a senior executive in the Crown Estates organisation, (not the Scotland rugby player of the same name!) and in our view his behaviour made him a star in our eyes.

We got away early to avoid the crowds and snuck past Cromer in the early morning. Thereafter it became more and more of a flog into the wind and at the stage where we were only making 1.5 knots we called it a day at Walcott. We had considered going on a few miles to the next marked RNLI station as we reasoned that there must be a slip there, but the rising wind dictated otherwise. Finding somewhere to camp started to look rather tricky until a couple, who let their field as a car park, said we could camp behind the cottage. This gave us access to water as well, so life took a turn for the better. Unfortunately the wind became, and stayed, ridiculous. The Kingfisher Restaurant provided a welcome change from 'expedition lunches' and we contributed mightily to the local economy by restocking from the village store.

Day 140 dawned and we got away after the usual trundle to get to the water: along the road, over the sea defences, back along the promenade and finally down yet more steps. We were getting good at this. We thought we had done well until we stopped as the tide turned against us and the wind rose again, but it turned out we had only covered 14 miles. The forecast of severe thunderstorms in the late afternoon did not encourage going on to Great Yarmouth, so we camped at California. This led to some hilarious misunderstandings both on the phone and when 'postcards from California' arrived at various people's houses! On the way, we passed the slip we had thought to continue to the previous day. It was a good job we had not done so; there had been a spot of coastal erosion at Happisburgh and the slip was no longer. Indeed, the road ended 30 feet in the air which would have been a definite challenge for landing kayaks and the RNLI inshore boat based there is currently taken by trailer to Walcott to launch. Our progress up the gravel at California was interrupted by an ice cream van. This was too good an opportunity to miss, especially when the ice cream man said 'I've read the words on the canoes – these are on me' – prompting another heartfelt 'thank you' from two tired paddlers!

As it turned out, we were stuck in California for six days. Very strong southerly winds and a series of violent thunderstorms kept us pinned down. We talked at length over our options for the trip as by now it was looking less and less likely that we would finish. Cath had to be back at work on November 1st, which meant we had to finish by mid-October. This gave us six weeks which would have been ample time given a decent run of weather, but that was something we had not had since the west coast of Scotland. The forecast from the Coastguard on a daily basis remained rubbish (and turned out to be so). One afternoon I had a long phone call from Steve Williams, who had attempted the circumnavigation in 2006, and he was astonished to find that we were still going. Possible temporary finish points came and went and we finally settled on trying to get to Plymouth, thus leaving a logical (and nice) 'lump' to finish in 2009. Having heard from her sister that her father was in hospital, Cath went to Plymouth for two days to see him, leaving me to guard the camp and gear. It was a cold and wet two days, but at last the forecast told of improving weather for Sunday 7 September. Coincidentally

Cath returned during the evening of the 6th, much happier for having seen her father. They both got a surprise when she had arrived at the house as her father had almost simultaneously returned from the hospital and neither was expecting to see the other there.

After a very wild and stormy night, the day broke quietly and calmly. In our rush to be away, both of us injured ourselves, Cath her shoulder and me my back, so it was a pair of sore and cross paddlers who passed Great Yarmouth and Lowestoft before reaching Southwold and the entrance to the River Blyth. We found a sheltered and discreet site next to the concrete buttresses of the river defences, cleared a lot of rubbish and got the tents up. Although both of us were sore, it had been a good day as we had passed the 1500 nautical miles point during the day! Monday 8 September was not a good day. I really should not have got on the water, I was in so much back pain. I had slipped as we got the boats off the sea wall at California, causing me to twist and lift at the same time as my arms were outstretched. This is a bad combination. Cath did all the lifting and carrying, and then fitted me into my boat. Going down to the river entrance was excruciatingly painful, with every small ripple causing my back to painfully spasm. Coming to my senses, we turned back in. The problem now was that I could not paddle hard enough to make progress against the outgoing tide, so Cath had to tow me back up the river. Getting back ashore and setting up the tents proved harder than the reverse and I needed a lot of help. Cath took the foot ferry to Southwold, coming back with the anti-inflammatory medication Brufen – to which the back pain responded. The forecast for the following day was yet again bad, so it looked as though my back would get a good rest before we got going again; this was something for which I was extremely grateful.

One day off turned into three as the wind got up and stayed up. Our chances of getting even to Plymouth seemed to recede by the day. On the plus side, my back responded to the medication and rest. We found the pub in Walberswick which gave good food but was expensive; the yacht club, which provided showers and cheap food; and the town of Southwold for cards and papers. Above the beach in Southwold is 'Gun Hill', a green terrace on which is an array of 17th century cannon. Although purely decorative, it was because of these cannon that the German High Seas Fleet bombarded the town during the First World War, so at the start of the Second World War they were promptly removed from the terrace and stored until the end of hostilities!

There were a lot of banners on the Walberswick side of the river saying 'Gord save us'. This made no sense initially until it was explained that the Prime Minister, then Gordon Brown, was holidaying in Southwold and the people of Walberswick wanted improved sea defences. It was tempting to observe that the appearance of Walberswick would seem to indicate a standard of living and income that could well afford to pay for their own sea defence improvements, if that was what they really wanted.

My feelings on Walberswick were not improved the following morning when over the sound of the wind I became aware of someone banging something on my boat to attract my attention. They succeeded. Putting my head out of the tent door I found a gentleman banging the boat with his walking stick, clearly not expecting a grey beard to appear! He appeared to think of himself as a retired colonel, blissfully unaware that he was addressing someone who categorically *was* a retired colonel! His observation that 'this isn't a campsite you know' only narrowly avoided igniting a fuse. Refraining from asking where the shower block was, I pointed out that we did not have a great deal of options given our position (could he not read the lettering on the side of the boats?) and the prevailing wind. He left, in a huff and muttering. A little while later, Cath appeared and said 'I didn't come out because I thought I might hit him!' Incidents like this annoyed both of us. We always cleaned the area we arrived in – here six carrier bags of rubbish had been taken to the bins in the car park – and only left footprints. It revealed to me also that I was becoming quite polarised in my approach to the trip: people either helped us, or they were against us. There was no middle ground. (I also thought that it showed that I had made a better transition to civilian life than some other ex-Army people…) Anyway… the wind dropped in the afternoon and all our aches and pains had subsided, so it looked like we would move again in the morning.

Although the wind dropped, the rain came and stayed, so after a fairly bad night's sleep we had a damp start to the day, paddling down to and past Sizewell nuclear power station. En route we passed Thorpeness, a small village clearly influenced either by Tobermory or Balamory with houses painted in an array of colours. Unfortunately the owners seemed not to have access to a tasteful paint palette as the selection of colours was rather harsh and they clashed somewhat. South of Aldeburgh, we pulled in at the base of a Martello tower (the most northerly one on the British mainland) and set up camp on a shingle ledge below the sea defences. The Martello towers, small round forts dating from the Napoleonic War era, originally stretched in a chain around the lower coast of England to defend against a possible French invasion. Many are now derelict although some have been converted to private dwellings and others remain as historic buildings. Thankfully the rain stopped, and the sea calmed as we had a late dinner and went to bed. All looked good for the morning and Orford Ness.

Saturday 13 September is best summed up by my diary entry:

'Crashing night – swell/surf dumping very heavily. Up to mist, but no wind and seems likely to burn off. But, as we got ready, the swell increased and so did the explosive dump – where the hell did that come from? It became rapidly apparent that we would have to be lucky, not good, to get two people off that beach unscathed, so it looked like another day beached (we've only paddled two days in the last 13!!!).'

Talking to the Coastguard revealed that beached we were, and would likely to be so for the following five days because of the approaching weather system… So we talked, and cried, and then I sent out the following text to those who had been following our progress:

'Well, five months and 1527 nautical miles later, our voyage ends in East Anglia. Full story later, but we are now in extrication mode. Don't worry, it feels good and is unquestionably the right thing to be doing! Thank you all for your support, we would not have done as well as we have without it. See you soon. Rowland.'

And so the adventure ended. Cath got sorted out very quickly and left for Plymouth to return in her car and collect me and all the gear. I was left alone to contemplate what I considered to be a shattered dream and failure. It was not a pleasant day and a half. A little while later I sent out the following to a close group of friends:

'A bit sad, but overwhelming feeling is glad to stop. Very tired! The fun went out of it a while back and it became an endurance and obstinacy test – and I've run out of both! Rowland.'

Return messages included:

'A very big congratulations on the 1527 nm. Well done to both of you. Looking forward to paddling with you soon. Colin and Gill.'

'You've done magnificently. See you sooner than we thought perhaps, but only after that beard has gone! Kate.'

'Well, good on you both I say. It's amazing what you have done and look forward to seeing you soon. Much love, Hannah.'

'Bummer. You've done well considering the weather though. Chris.'

'So sorry about the trip, but what an achievement given what the weather has thrown at you! Hope you're both OK. Wendy.'

'Sorry to get your news this morning, but you sound OK about it all. Quite some feat anyway! Lucy.'

'Amazing achievement to get so far against the odds. Well done the pair of you. You just happened to have picked probably the worst year ever! Certainly in terms of strong wind it must be! Not to mention lack of sunlight, and rain! Tim.'

And from one who had 'been there, done that':

'When the weather is against you there's not a lot you can do about it, but what a great trip. Look forward to a chat. Steve Williams.'

Norfolk Lunch Break. (C.Tanner)

The end of a dream… (C. Tanner)

Aftermath

The immediate aftermath was horrible; I am under no illusion that I was nice to be with. Very few people seemed to understand that I could not view the expedition as anything other than a failure. When I looked at the back of the small scale GB map we were using to record our overall progress, I saw not the thick black line of felt tip that showed what we had done, but only the untouched southern section that taunted me with its unmarked status. I had spent most of my life in a family and then a system that only recognised success and achievement. Trying and not succeeding was failing, pure and simple. I had sunk a lot of emotional capital into circumnavigating Britain, and my ethic was that that meant a continuous journey, from start to finish. Nothing else counted; it might be described as 'paddling around', but it was not, to me, a circumnavigation. That was the style that had been set from the first circumnavigation, and that was the standard to which I aspired, and was to be measured by.

For nearly two months I did not paddle and I actually seriously considered giving up kayaking altogether and selling my boats and gear. And then one morning, two friends turned up on the doorstep and said 'get your gear, we're going paddling'. It was not an option I had any choice in! The following day, the same thing happened again, and by the end of that second day, I had rediscovered the gentle joys of fun paddling in good company – 'thank you' Colin and Gill, you really did make a significant difference.

I was less enamoured of being at a sea kayak symposium the following year as the attitude of some people clearly reflected the 'succeed or fail' ethos of some of the 'inner group' on Anglesey. Interestingly, when I was given a rainy Monday morning slot to talk about the trip, those who attended described it as the best presentation of the symposium, primarily because of my honesty about the aftermath, but also because I was prepared to talk about what really happened, not just the 'PR gloss' version. My attitude to some people whom I had previously thought of as friends changed over that nine month period, not always for the better. Some people seem able to walk away from major events like an attempted circumnavigation, whether successful or not, and return to 'normal life' without any apparent effect. I am apparently in the other category – forever changed by the experience, but whether for better or worse is for others to judge, not me.

My biggest regret was temporarily losing contact with Cath. When we returned in her car to Plymouth, she dropped me at my brother's house and we went our separate ways. We spoke occasionally, but that ease of long companionship and shared endeavour was gone. To me Cath was the mainstay of the whole thing. Without her, it would probably not have got off the ground, and it certainly would not have gone on for so long. I am certain that had she truly exercised her free will, she would have left the trip somewhere in north eastern Scotland. As it was, she stuck with me for most of the east coast (not the prettiest or most rewarding section of the coastline!) purely because I wanted to carry on. I know I must have been hard to be with, and horribly unsympathetic at times, yet still she carried on. I owe her a debt I can never repay, but I was not surprised at her seemingly wanting to walk away from me and the aftermath and leave it in the past. How did she feel about it all? At the time I did not know, because we had never sat down and talked it through. Fortunately that was to change in a few years time.

Interregnum

I never intended to try and complete the trip. To do so seemed in some way to accept the validity of an 'alternative definition' of a circumnavigation, something I could not accept then and to this day something with which I still have difficulty. 2009 saw me attending both the Anglesey and Scottish Sea Kayak symposiums, and then building a skin-on-frame rolling kayak under the watchful eye of American paddlers Turner Wilson and Cheri Perry.

Part of the disincentive was the South East. I was born in north Kent and my memories of the coast there and round to the Isle of Wight were not a basis for returning to paddle it. Consequently, the only section that attracted could broadly be described as 'the South West'. If I went and did that as a complete section, the likelihood of finishing the whole coastline by paddling the south eastern corner was vanishingly small. So, for some reason, the whole of the south went untouched as a project...

Late in 2009 I had to undergo a hernia operation, and the painful aftermath of that effectively kept me out of paddling for a year. It was late 2010 before I stopped being aware of the dull ache and scar pains when I picked up a boat. And then, late one evening, over a glass of whisky, Barry Bramley asked the loaded question 'have you ever thought of finishing your trip?'...

PART TWO
The Last Quarter?

Starting Again

The itch was definitely there; the problems in my head over what constituted a circumnavigation had not gone away, but they were less strident. More insistent was the thought 'it would be a shame not to do the rest…' Also at the back of my mind was that I seemed to be the only person having problems with the thought of finishing. More than one person said 'just go and do it!' And so I started to warm to the idea of completion.

Barry Bramley is another paddler in the Oban area, a retired firefighter, and someone with whom I paddled a lot. His question over the glass of whisky was only the final push on a door well on its way to being open. We looked at each other, and then at our diaries. I estimated that six weeks would be more than enough to complete the remainder, particularly as it would be reasonable to assume that the weather would not be as continuously bad as it had been in 2008. In retrospect it would probably have helped if we had both pencilled in the same six weeks into our diaries! We did not, but that only became apparent much nearer to the start and by then various other commitments conspired to give us only between four and five weeks for the trip. Still sufficient, in average conditions… I did think about talking again to Cath, both to see if she was interested in finishing off the trip and also to check if she had any objection to me finishing it with someone else. In the event what little contact we did have reassured me on both accounts – and to this day she has expressed no burning desire to close the circle. Circumnavigations are very personal affairs.

Some things were easy: I still had full chart coverage, and Barry had access to the map coverage, but we both needed boats. My Explorer had been hammered in 2008, and subsequent use had involved a couple of rock dodging moments that were 'dodging' light and 'rock' heavy! The extent of repairs that had been done did not bode well for another extended expedition unless we were prepared to carry out heavy 'running repairs' en route. Barry was happy with his boat, until he unexpectedly found a major wear hole and, on closer inspection, further evidence of age and decrepitude.

After a lot of thought, we settled on using Valley Sea Kayak's (VSK) Etains. These were a new model, but one with a developing good reputation. Jason Buxton of VSK was very generous to us, so less damage to our bank balances was inflicted than might otherwise have been. He also, in light of the short time to the 'off', personally delivered them to Penrith where in the best tradition of Berlin spy swaps we 'met in the middle' and then went on our separate return trips! We both decided to use UK-made dry bibs; these seemed good to start with but failed spectacularly in use (of which more later). One thing that had changed for me was that a friend in Sweden, Sara Wagner, had started to make Greenland paddles of an advanced design and built in carbon fibre. The paddles were called 'BlackLight' (because they were black in colour, and did not weigh very much) and I had had the opportunity to try a set at the Anglesey Symposium. Rather taken by them, I arranged with Sara to use them for the remainder of the circumnavigation. That paddle has stood up well, being in almost constant use ever since.

The paddling plan was relatively straightforward: return to Aldeburgh and put on the water, heading firstly to Orford Ness and ultimately Ilfracombe.

Back at Aldeburgh in 2011.

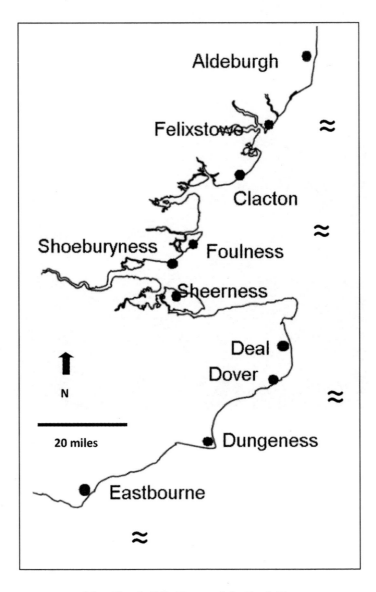

Map 10 – Suffolk, Essex and the South East

Through the Bat Hole, east Dorset.

Furthest west in 2011 - the Bill of Portland.

Sky signs warning of the impending storms.

After the storm – the day we left Looe.

The aftermath of landing through seaweed at Fowey.

Along the west side of the Lizard.

Waiting for the tide to turn at Land's End.

Passing Cape Cornwall – the last corner.

Fistral Beach in atypical conditions.

Boscastle.

Three miles to go!

Entering Ilfracombe – journey over.

The finishing team at Ilfracombe.

Reunited with Cath at Ilfracombe.

Suffolk Shingle, Essex Mud

And so it was that at midday Thursday 12 May 2011, Barry, Carol and I were on the beach at Aldeburgh packing two boats for what was intended to be '2011 – The Last Quarter'. It was a rather odd feeling being there again, and not an entirely comfortable one. I had never expected to see the Martello tower again, but at least this time the winds were gentle, and in our favour, as was the tide, and the sea was calm. Leaving involved the usual horribly emotional 'good bye' and then we were off, being swept rewardingly south by the tide. The boats were 'trip start heavy', so our plan was only to get south of Orford Ness and then find a site to camp. This we did, after 11 miles, at Bawdsey. The location was not the most scenic being a corner sandbank on seaweed under the sea defences, but it was sheltered and would definitely do. There was the usual rummaging around in the boats as it takes about four days before things settle into a customary place, and then we started to settle into 'expedition routine'.

Friday the 13th was better than it might have been; we started into both a cold wind and an adverse tide, but we snuck around the coast until the entrance to Felixstowe. I had always considered this to be one of the potential crux points, but in reality traffic was light to non-existent, so we scooted across the rather bumpy channel and then fought our way into the wind to the Naze, where we had lunch standing on a mudflat. On after lunch, with both of us tired, we reached a point just east of Clacton and ended up camping at the top of the beach. Clacton was a possible jumping off point for a long crossing south direct to the north Kent coast. This was not an attractive option as the wind was fiercely westerly. The plan we developed was to follow the coast to the River Crouch and then pass the Foulness Ranges as close as possible, endeavouring not to be blown out to sea. That also meant we would pass the range on a Sunday, which being a non-firing day, rather simplified things.

The next section, down to the River Crouch, passed in a day of two halves. We firstly caught the morning tide (4 a.m.) along the coast until we could make a very sporting, and wet, crossing to the south side of the Blackwater. Here we landed at high water, and then stood and watched as the tide receded from view at a fast rate. It would be about 9 p.m. before the water returned for the second phase of the day, so we settled down in the sun for an afternoon's rest, neither of us having slept at all well the night before. We also tried to dry out our kit; the so-called dry bibs were nothing of the sort and both of us were wet inside them. It was not condensation, so water was getting in somewhere. Later in the trip, on one occasion Barry actually emptied a significant amount of water from his booties at the end of a day – to the accompaniment of a few choice words on quality control and design. One of the socks on my bibs had holed on the first day, so now was a good time to break out the repair goo and also sort that out. The mouth of the Blackwater is very rural Essex with extensive views of mudflats. Some of the characters who passed by could have come straight from the pages of a novel by Charles Dickens or played as extras in a BBC production of one. Barry went for a walk at one stage and was captured by members of a commune, only being allowed to escape after having drunk much tea and eaten many cakes! I whiled away part of the afternoon by working out when the water might reappear; it was very satisfying to find that the actual time was only 10 minutes from that I had calculated. Night fell as the water returned, so we had a dark paddle down to and into the River Crouch. En route a suicidal fish startled me by throwing itself at the side of the kayak, impacting with a mighty crash. We found our way by finger tip into the Crouch and discovered a break in the sea defences leading to a small sandbank where we got ashore and gratefully put up our tents. It had been a long day, despite the break, and we were both tired, but at least we were in position to pass the ranges on the morning tide.

The best laid plans... went awry the following morning when at 6 a.m., having brushed my teeth, I coughed and went again into atrial fibrillation. Shades of Cape Wrath! In retrospect it was easy to see where the trail began: two or three bad nights' sleep, pushing too hard at the start to get into position to pass the ranges and, almost certainly, dehydration. Anyway, the tactical response was to take an extra dose of the usual medication, retire to the tent and lie down, crossing my fingers that it would revert of its own accord to a normal rhythm. (It did, late that evening. Had it not done so, a slow paddle to Burnham-on-Crouch and the search for a hospital would have been the only option.) During the day I exchanged text messages with a doctor friend in Dublin, Jason Horan, who found himself in the not entirely enviable position of trying to manage me by remote control. Barry spent the day bird watching and finding a source for water. He was as pleased as I was when everything went back to normal that evening. We did now have a problem though: the Foulness Ranges.

Everything remained normal overnight, and both of us got a reasonable night's sleep, but the advice from Jason was to rest up the whole day and seriously rehydrate. Speaking to Range Control revealed a major problem as the ranges were in use every day until 4 p.m. That did not easily work with the tides. Going around the outside of Foulness Island was a non-starter because of the westerly winds, so we looked at all the possibilities, including having to stop! Part of the problem was that for some reason I had fixated on getting across the Thames as well as passing the range in the next 'hop'. Whilst I was still pondering how to do this without waiting for the following weekend, Barry suddenly said 'why don't we just stop at Shoeburyness for the night?' Some things are, in retrospect, blindingly obvious! So now the plan we worked on was to use the morning tide on the following day to get to the very edge of the back of the range and then wait until the range closed. We would then get as far as we could through the range before we lost water as the tide fell, wait until it returned, and then continue to Shoeburyness.

And so it happened:

'Rather bizarre day… Lazy start, waiting for the midday tide and then rode that to the entrance to the Roach, south of Wallsea Island. Sat there (thank goodness no rain!) until the range closed, then (after a muddy relaunch on a par with the Gironde) pootled until stopped by a lack of water. Oddly, we got through the bridge to the outside and then got totally dried. Another long, muddy wait (including cooking in the cockpit and having a cuckoo fly over me) until 9.30 p.m. when the water finally started to come back. Even so, it took ages to get deep enough to paddle. Funny and frustrating at the same time. Anyway then had an 'interesting' night paddle to Shoeburyness, found a beach outside the range and stopped (at 1 a.m.)'

I found out afterwards that this was an option taken by at least two other circumnavigating parties when faced with the same westerly winds and open ranges problem. At one point as we stopped in yet another slowly filling pool of muddy water, both Barry and I simultaneously commented on the number of lights we could see on a refinery tower on the north Kent coast. The more lights we could see, the more we were finally rising with the tide! The final approach to Shoeburyness is marked with several major obstacles in the water including posts, fences and isolated towers, few of them lit. I had a major problem – my eyesight, once so good, was now badly affected by a cataract in my right eye. As a result I was not able to see very much at night and Barry had to keep giving me warnings of things I was about to hit that I had not seen at all.

There was no rush in the morning as the water would not return until midday, and we were tempted to sit tight as the wind was kicking up a fierce sea state in the Thames estuary. Whilst passing the time, we found a small corner shop whose brilliant owner not only sourced nearly all the items on the shopping list, but let us recharge our electrics as well. A chandlery sold me a small gas canister (for some reason I was rather low on gas) and also recommended we move two miles east to Thorpe Bay where there was a sailing club – 'they'll look after you'. And so we did, and so they did. It was a very wet and lumpy passage, with a downright dangerous landing onto a raised slipway at the end, but the rewards were showers, clean clothes and recharged electrics. Thank you, Thorpe Bay Yacht Club. It would again be a late start the next day, despite a very favourable forecast, because yet again we could only just see the water… it goes out a long way in Essex!

Dawn launch in Essex

Landing at Shellness Point, Kent.

South East England

It was not a terribly good night. I think we were camped close to the lay-by used by the local drug dealers, with cars coming and going until long into the small hours. And then, just as it all seemed to be quietening down, there came the less than delightful sound of someone vomiting on the pavement. The joys of urban camping! One incident in the morning highlighted a difference between the experience of 2008 and this year. Barry does not take enforced idleness very well, so had wandered off into the shopping area of town. He enjoyed a coffee and a pastry and then returned in just enough time to pack up his boat before launching onto the Thames. I would have appreciated being brought back a pastry rather than just being told about it! Cath and I had always done that for each other, it was just one of those unsaid 'done things'. It was a small thing, by no means significant, but it did underline that this time it was going to be a different sort of trip. Sufficient water returned to let us get going at 1 p.m. and we had a straightforward crossing of the Thames to Sheerness. After stopping to put on paddling jackets as it looked warmer than it was, we ran with the tide until Shell Point on the west side of the River Swale. We left landing about 10 minutes too late and had a horrendous drag of the boats through mud as a result. At one point Barry lost a boot and all we could do was lean on each other and laugh hysterically. The houses on the point are, as we subsequently found out, a private estate but all were empty and we effectively landed in a ghost town. We found a tap that worked, so at least we could wash off the mud, and there being not many other options, we set up camp on 'the village green'.

This was another of those places which, like the empty holiday homes in the empty villages of coastal Wales and Scotland, made me re-evaluate my thoughts on second home ownership. Faced with the reality of houses standing empty for the majority of the year, it just did not seem right when put against the inability of most of the indigenous local coastal population to buy a home in their own community.

We had to wait until after lunch the following day for the tide to return (we did not fancy the 3 a.m. alternative) and in the interim were visited by the estate caretaker. The initial approach – 'you can't camp here' – changed somewhat when he found out what we were doing. He also appreciated that we were not dragging our boats back out across the mud to meet the incoming tide! That day saw us pass Whitstable, Herne Bay and Reculver along some spectacular mud-sculpture cliffs. We eventually pulled in just west of Margate as this seemed to be the only option before rounding North Foreland, camping just above the sea defences and attracting many curious visitors. The plan was to be on the water for 5 a.m. to catch the tide east to the third of the four corners of my paddle around Britain.

We were up and away early, so we had an atmospheric run into the dawn passing Ramsgate and then North Foreland. Near the headland was an amphitheatre built into the cliffs, so we were serenaded by the Stereophonics at full throttle as we passed. I doubt they were playing live at that hour of the morning, so it was probably a sound check for a later concert. I hope it was not as loud when heard from landward. As we crossed towards Deal, the wind got up and the day turned into an unpleasant flog into a cold wind. Beach breaks relieved the monotony of paddling along shingle banks, but gave Barry an entertaining moment each time he landed. His demonstrations of aquabatics definitely kept me entertained! The small chalk cliffs before St Margaret's Bay were enjoyable but round them we caught the full force of the wind, so we landed through small but snarling surf to look for somewhere to camp. The car park had numerous 'no camping' signs, so we hid round the back of a shelter that had been built in the form of an upturned boat. This gave us grass for the tents and only a short walk to the toilets and a pub. All of a sudden we had company; Jake Monk, a kayak paddler who decided that we looked like we needed adopting. I was given a lift to the nearest village store (it was some distance) and then back again, for which we were very grateful. Thereafter we sampled the delights of lemon sole washed down by Kentish ale before retiring to our (flat) beds.

Gales kept us firmly beached for the next three days, and there is not a great deal to do in the narrow confines of St Margaret's Bay. We sorted out food resupply and one of the pub staff got me a new, large, gas canister. The house at the end of the green sward area was apparently owned at some point by Noel Coward. It certainly looked the part for the house parties of that set. The cliffs are riddled with tunnels from the First and Second World Wars, but all you could see was the initial few metres inside. It was tempting to explore further, but would probably not have been terribly sensible.

On the second day we took it in turns to walk up the cliff path to visit the monument to the Dover Patrol. This was a force of small vessels operating in the Straits in the First World War. From the top, we still could not see across to France as the visibility was so limited. That unfortunately did not stop our mobile phones deciding we were in France, so calls home became rather expensive as a result. On the third day Barry walked into, and explored Deal whilst I opted for the other approach and hid in the tent from the wind and read. Unfortunately, having long legs, my feet stuck out of the tent and I ended up with some patterned sunburn as a result; that was sore. The early forecast on the third day was promising for a move on the morrow, but by the time the evening forecast came around it was not so clear cut. The thought of being stuck in St Margaret's Bay for a fourth day brought near despair to the pair of us, although I did note in my diary that 'we've only been here three days, which is peanuts by 2008's standards!'

We woke to a nice day and a radically improved forecast, so we got rapidly away, reaching the entrance to Dover Harbour really quite quickly. Dover Control agreed with our plan of coming in the eastern entrance and going out of the western one, thus enabling us to avoid the standing patch of very confused water outside the breakwater. The skipper of a P&O cross-Channel ferry then covered himself in glory by volunteering to leave by the west entrance – not his scheduled exit – giving us more time and space to get into the harbour. We were very grateful! After Dover comes the Channel Tunnel entrance, which kicks up a sea state even in good weather because of the extensive sea defences, and the entrance to

Folkestone harbour, which was oddly quiet and easy to pass. The next two critical areas are the small arms ranges at Hythe and Lydd. These are constantly in use by day and night, so a bit of planning is required to get around them. In the event, we just paddled offshore of Hythe, getting wet and cold in the process, and on down to Dungeness. The wind increased as we approached the very tip, so we crashed ashore through the diagonal surf and surveyed the scene. Well, if we thought Essex was 'odd', this took 'oddness' to a whole new level. The area was like a modern archaeology site with rusted industrial and fishing gear strewn around. What we did not appreciate at the time, and had no means of so doing, was that the whole area was the berthing slips for the local fishing fleet. So, we set up camp in a small hollow in the shingle, doing our best to remain inconspicuous. Other than the wind, it was very quiet, almost eerie one might say…

The forecast Force 8 gale hit overnight, followed by a Force 9 the next day. My diary records, laconically, 'bloody windy today'. We resorted to ferreting out some fish crates to fill with shingle, tying the tents down as well as we could; they still shook.

We were awoken at 3.30 a.m. the following day by the sounds of the nearest fishing boat being pushed down the beach by a bulldozer. It was clearly still a working fleet, if much reduced in activity. Once the boat had gone, everything settled down until an old chap came along. He was mightily annoyed that we were there and had used the fish crates to hold ourselves down. I put on my most diplomatic face and gradually talked him down, after which normal inactivity returned. The forecast remained bad, Force 6 westerly, but the wind was dropping and everything seemed to be calming down early. I walked to the nearest shop and then caught the bus back, visiting the local lifeboat station en route. The coxswain reckoned the weather would stay fair for the day, so he spoke to the Lydd range control to find out when it would stop firing. As it was a Friday, the answer he received was '4.30 at the latest!' I scooted back to the camp and we got ourselves ready to go, intending to get to the eastern range boundary then check to see what was the state of play with the range. It felt good to get away from Dungeness; another place on the coast I have no desire to revisit. I cannot repeat what Barry said (he being a plain-speaking Yorkshireman!)

The outfall from the Dungeness nuclear power station was kicking up a weird sea (would there be any other sort around here?) so we crept along the inside line, making sure we did not get taken in by the swell and surf. Landing at the range boundary was unnecessarily exciting as dumping surf and steep shingle beaches do not make a good combination. After walking to the boundary lookout tower (the red range flag was still flying) and discovering no-one was at home, matters were exacerbated by finding that firing had already stopped and we need not have landed at all! As a result we re-launched, getting soaked again, and crossed the bay to the River Rother and Rye Harbour. Much as with Scottish sand dunes and Lincolnshire mudflats, shingle beaches have little to offer in the way of scenic beauty, and they all seem to take an age to traverse. We were bored and cold as we pulled in to the mouth of the Rother; an abortive landing and search for a campsite on the east shore was followed by a entertaining landing on the west side. All was going well, the tents being set up in a small hollow in the lee of an old Second World War fortification, until officialdom turned up in the form of a nature reserve warden. (We were clearly and unarguably outside the reserve boundary!) The usual start to the conversation 'you can't camp here' was trumped by my 'paddling around Britain in aid of the RNLI', with an unsubtle sub-text of 'we're not moving!' As I pointed out, we were both too old, and more to the point too tired, to engage in riotous behaviour. A long telephone conversation with 'The Boss' ensued (whilst we carried on with dinner – 'we are NOT moving') and we were at last allowed, reluctantly, to stay. It was probably a good job that none of us realised that we would be stuck there for three days by wind.

Next day Barry turned on the charm at the nearby caravan site and we were allowed to use the showers and washing facilities, so at least we got clean. Rye Harbour has a café, a pub and a small store and not much else. We became familiar with all three. The restaurant in the caravan site did extremely good bacon baps for breakfast, so that became a theme. Barry explored and went bird watching and I watched birds and read. We thought we might move on the third day, but it dawned with thick fog and the (changed) forecast of more westerly wind. Over the course of the morning, the fog went and the wind came, so we stayed. I noted in my diary that we had now lost nine days of 19, which is by far a much worse ratio than Cath and I had suffered in 2008. Finishing the last quarter in 2011 was starting to look a little unlikely.

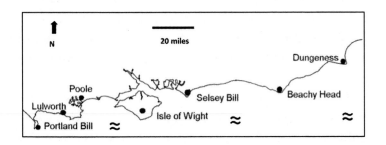

Map 11 – South Coast Central.

South Coast Central

At last, on Tuesday 31 May, we got away:

'Good weather, good forecast, good breakfast and off. Cliffs to Hastings good, thereafter scenery less so. Finally got to Sovereign Harbour at Eastbourne. Tired. Grumpy. 20 nm.'

Landing at Sovereign Harbour at our first attempt proved horribly muddy and fruitless, so we re-launched and went to the outside. Here we landed on near-vertical shingle, having a really hard time getting up the beach to find a shelf on which to camp. There was the option of two – 'would sirs like the upper or lower shelf?' – but a check of the tidetables and a bit of measuring Barry's height against the side of the beach led us to opt for 'high'. (Which was just as well, as at 3.30 a.m. the lower shelf was under water.) A group of what transpired to be German exchange students on a language course entertained themselves at the far end of the beach, but then decided that being a nuisance at our end was more fun. Stones landing on and around the tents incurred Barry's wrath, and they came very close to getting some very rude German words flung at them in return (I have not forgotten *all* my German!) Eventually they left. In passing, we both thought that the housing development at Sovereign Harbour was close to, if not the worst example of modern housing we had ever seen. I knew it looked bad from landward; from the sea it is incomparably worse.

It was good to wake to a flat sea and blue sky; once again it was time to get out of Dodge! I did not enjoy paddling the seafront at Eastbourne, passing the pier, bandstand and RNLI shop; there were too many memories associated with them. My parents lived for many years in Eastbourne, with the RNLI being my mother's adopted charity. She raised many thousands of pounds and died 'in harness' whilst fundraising during flag week. We were suckered by the sky into not bothering to put on our paddle jackets, and were rewarded by a lumpy sea and a headwind as we rounded Beachy Head; the cliffs here are far more impressive than the famed 'White Cliffs of Dover', which are low-lying and scruffy in comparison. Stopping at Birling Gap, we got dressed properly and then demonstrated excellent style in getting off yet another steep shingle beach. Perhaps we were finally getting the hang of these infernal pieces of beach geography. The cliffs to Cuckmere Haven are the Seven Sisters, all very scenic but Barry was rather put off by the number of unclothed gentlemen who disported themselves on the small pocket beaches at the base; I assured him that we did not have to land on this section! Re-launching after lunch proved trying as both of us hung up on shelves, getting stones jammed in our skeg boxes as a result. This meant landing, clearing the boxes then launching yet again; all very tedious with an awkward cross-current combining with the outflow from the river to create an awkward sea. Our target became Newhaven, the lure being the marina marked on the chart, as we were in dire need of a shower. The journey was better than the arrival. After fruitless and aggravating discussions with various people (prompting us to ask just what it is about the south east which makes some people so unpleasant?), we gave up on Newhaven and camped outside the port on a spit of land, seemingly miles from anywhere. It did, however, give us close-up views of the ferry as it entered the harbour. Some late night anglers came down to try their luck later in the evening but we were undisturbed. It had been a hard won 13 miles, with a depressing finish, but all this was put to one side when I got the news that Ginny had gained a 2:1 in zoology from Glasgow. Big smiles all round!

In contrast, the following day was really good. We enjoyed a blue sky, no wind and some impressive chalk cliff scenery to Brighton. En route we passed the Greenwich Meridian marker, which was about 100 metres out of position according to the GPS. Lunch at Brighton was 'different', as we had to find enough space to get ashore between the sunbathers. A long hot afternoon then followed until we ran out of tide, water and enthusiasm at East Preston, incurring the longest beach walk yet to find a place on the gravel for the night. The trolley came into its own here, and it was worth carrying it even if only for this landing. It was clearly an affluent area as the local shops included boutiques, poodle parlours, home laundry services and on-call cleaners. The owner of the house we camped near did look at us rather quizzically, but once he found out what we were doing, he smiled, returned to the house and came back out with two cold beers – apologising that had he not been leaving the following morning we would have been invited in for dinner. The contrast with Newhaven could not have been more marked, and it seemed to us there was a very real divide in attitudes east and west of the Greenwich meridian. Later in the evening a friend from the Lake District, Kav, came to visit us as a respite from teaching an industrial rope access course in Chichester; a pleasant interlude for all of us.

It was a gentle start as the water was rather a long way away, but thereafter we moved very quickly along the coast in front of a Force 5-6 wind. A wet but exhilarating day for once. Lunch at Bognor provided yet another horrible landing and launching and we then played dodge the overfalls across to Selsey Bill, rounding this at about 7-8 knots, slaloming between moored boats at high speed and close quarters. We paid for this by having a very uninteresting gravel beach section to Wittering, which took a long time to reach, and then a vicious little crossing to Hayling Island. The streams running out of Chichester Harbour entrance were at maximum rate and we fought mightily but still lost ground. As a result, we had to walk the boats in the edge of the water 400 metres back towards the lifeboat station where we set up camp on the grass. By this stage of the trip, we had given up asking about camping and just did it. Hayling Island Sailing Club rather reluctantly allowed us to wash both ourselves and our kit... I got the impression that we were 'lowering the tone'. In the evening Carol arranged to visit early in the morning; the tides were all wrong for a move until 2 p.m. and the weather was in any event questionable.

Whilst Barry went walkabout in the morning, I entertained a stream of passers-by. These included a local lady, Gillian, who kidnapped all our dirty clothes, took them home, washed

Rounding Beachy Head.

Passing Hurst Castle in the west Solent.

and returned them. Clearly an inhabitant 'west of the meridian'! Thank you! Carol came and resupplied us with food, maps and charts and then, after the usual grim farewell, we set off west into the Solent. We crossed between the forts at Horsesands, after pausing (not comfortably) to let an enormous liner depart from Portsmouth. We passed Ryde and its hovercraft and headed for Cowes. There is a marked difference in paddling these heavily congested waters compared to the quiet of our home on the west coast of Scotland. We were by far the smallest things around and probably nearly invisible to most other water users. As a result there was a constant stream of commentary – 'liner far right', 'yachts coming from rear left', 'motorboat leaving that slip on the left' – from both of us as we made sure nothing escaped our awareness.

We did not expect to see the number of 'No' signs on the foreshore, and it took a long time to find a spot apparently not inside any form of forbidden zone. Much of the foreshore here lies in the grounds of Osborne House, once Queen Victoria's family home, and access is zealously controlled. Of course, as we set up the tents we were challenged from seaward... Wading out to the motorboat, I explained what I was doing and rather emphatically stated that I was so tired I was not moving. The wardens, thankfully, gave us approval for a 'one night, away early' stay. It had been, in many respects, a good day and I had passed the '1750 miles Round Britain' point two miles before we pulled in.

We paid a price to the sea gods for staying in a forbidden zone. The tide was rather high early in the morning and sent waves crashing into the base of the wall, showering the tents at intervals. However, we were away early, crossing the entrance to the River Medina at Cowes (passing a US registered tall ship, the Bounty) and then headed out into the flow to take us down the western arm of the Solent. My diary records that this section was occasionally 'sporting'… We debated for quite a while about going into Lymington as the weather was peculiar; it could not seem to make up its mind whether to be vile or just overcast. The dilemma was that outside the Solent we would be back into the land of steep shingle, and if the weather deteriorated that would mean hard landings.

In the end, the thought of trying to find another campsite inside the Solent was worse than keeping our weather fingers crossed, so we ran down the west arm, passed Hurst Fort and went out into the Channel. The tide race at Hurst Fort was benign, being fast and flat, but the payment extracted was near-zero visibility; we could only just make out the Needles at the western tip of the Isle of Wight. The long lazy swell stole my boat from the steep shingle beach at the lunch break when my back was turned, so we had to re-launch Barry in 'fetch' mode. Needless to say, he made the most of rescuing my boat! The coast from there to Christchurch harbour is manicured mudstone, as opposed to the manicured chalk cliffs of Sussex. It is still not terribly scenic on a damp overcast grey day, however. We sneaked into the harbour and just decided to pull up on the beach and camp next to the public toilets, amid a whole collection of beach huts. We were mildly challenged later in the evening, but no real effort was made to get us to move. Of more concern was that both of us were now permanently wet. Both our, admittedly old, jackets were letting in water and the new salopettes were not slowing it down much. It was on this evening that Barry actually emptied out significant amounts of water from each foot...

The morning dawned with the patter of mild drizzle, but the forecast was fair, so we planned to move. Breakfast was enlivened by watching fishermen shooting nets from the shore and then rowing them around a section of water to be hand-dragged back in. They were after sea trout, but as we watched they also caught, tagged and released a fairly large salmon. We paddled west under low cliffs, passing Bournemouth (groomed beaches and colour-coordinated beach huts) to have lunch at Sandbanks, just before Poole Harbour. For what is reputed to be the most expensive real estate in the country, it frankly looked rather scruffy from seaward. Dodging the ferry, we crossed Studland Bay to arrive at Old Harry Rocks, the Jurassic coast, stacks, arches and sea birds. Barry's comment was 'at last – after three weeks – SCENERY!' I think he had had enough of the low-lying badlands and shingle.

The whole thing got even better once off Swanage as we hit the limestone cliffs leading west. With the exception of the tide race and overfalls of St Alban's Head, which gave me a flashback to 2008 when saints' heads equalled rough waters, the sea was relatively quiet. This meant we could get in amongst all the back corners and into the nooks and crannies. It was a pleasant afternoon paddle, ending in the idyllic location of Chapman's Pool. Here we found two small grass shelves to camp on; only after putting up the tents did we spot the 'no camping, no fires' notice. The evening was the best yet, but the forecast for the morning was 50/50, with a wind warning for 'later'. Our provisional plan was to get up very early to catch the morning tide, head along the Lulworth range area, and pull in afterwards at Lulworth Cove for a late breakfast. Well, that was the plan.

Given the military adage that 'no plan survives contact with the enemy', this is what I wrote the following evening:

'Interesting day… what is it about ranges? Awoke 5 a.m. – flat calm. Forecast at 5.18 favourable – F3-4 SW increasing 4-5 later (i.e. after 12 hours). Up quickly, aiming for breakfast in Lulworth. Slow passing Kimmeridge Ledges, then the wind started and the stream turned early… Off Worbarrow Tout we got a good kicking and crossing Worbarrow Bay was hard, very hard. Getting more and more tired (no breakfast). Off Mupe Rocks (only 1 nm to go) sea got right up and I realised I had not got the puff. Told Barry, who looked startled.'

I had run out of energy. I had a choice. I could struggle on towards Lulworth, possibly provoking my heart condition and quite likely needing a real rescue, or turn in to the Arish Mell beach and cover myself with embarrassment with the Range staff. We turned towards the beach.

'As we turned in, the Range Safety boat appeared. We were invited for a chat, during which they suggested getting the boats on board their vessel – no chance. So they organised a reception committee, and we landed, to be met by range wardens. Very friendly and helpful (albeit the piss was extracted mightily when they found out what I had been in my previous life). Boats stashed at the top of the beach and we were then taken to Range Control. Here the mick was again taken, but the Commandant was amused, giving us a very welcome cup of tea. Very tired. Given the late arrival of a unit for the range, decided to recover boats on a flat-bed truck, so back to the beach and load. Then taken to Durdle Door campsite, to discover no realistic beach access [it is at the top of a very high cliff!]. So, down to Lulworth Cove and hope! Found Christine Miller in her fish shop, who said 'of course you can camp behind here' – thank you! Boats delivered and dropped off, then the recovery started. Tents up, gear drying, electrics charging and then up to the café for a full breakfast – yum! Then a resting day, sending out a long text message to explain what had happened. Pub meal in the evening. Moved 8 nm today – but only paddled 7 nm!'

Christine's husband Joe is a local fisherman, and he appeared late in the afternoon, grinning broadly. He had heard all of our little adventure develop on the radio. He did say that the tide had turned early and the wind had got up far earlier than forecast, so we did not feel entirely as though we had been wrong to set out in the morning. It would, however, be the last time I got on the water without having breakfast. Part of the text message I sent out provoked a lot of responses. I had said that when we got back on the water, we would have to turn east and paddle back to Mupe Rocks, before turning west again and resuming our journey. Some people had difficulty with that as a concept, but I could not face the thought of eventually having paddled the entire coastline – except for the one mile between Mupe Rocks and Lulworth Cove. The itch that would create just did not bear thinking about!

We were beached for the next two days as a series of

westerlies blew through. The good thing was that we had sunshine so could dry out all the gear, wash clothes and carry out the minor repairs we needed. The downside was that it was expensive buying meals in cafés and pubs, and we had a sneaking feeling that we were perhaps outstaying our welcome a little. As with many places in the south, camping in Lulworth Cove is 'forbidden'… A moment of light relief occurred when Christine's niece came out of the fish shop with the phone in her hand and said 'is one of you called Barry?' It transpired that Wendy, Barry's wife, had 'googled' 'fish shop Lulworth Cove', found only the one and rang the number on the off chance it was the right one! On the second day we doubted our decision not to move until a Force 6 westerly came in late morning; the whitecaps and sea state outside the bay were spectacular. Late in the afternoon a friend of mine, Kirsti, and one of her friends (both BA pilots) turned up to visit us and then cooked us a meal on the beach. This was a chilly but very welcome experience. The forecast for the next two days kept on changing, so it was hard to make a definite decision to go. Portland Bill is the next crux point, and after that comes the long extent of the steep shingle of Chesil Beach. We would need a clear weather window to get along that as it turns into a definite no-landing zone with any heavy swell and surf.

After some indecision, we left the following day; paddling back east to Mupe Rocks, then turning around and re-starting our westward journey. The section of coastline we paddled in the morning was spectacular. We passed through the great arch of Durdle Door and through the small cleft of the Bat Hole in the cliffs of the Bat Head, so it was after a good morning that we landed on the eastern edge of Weymouth Bay for lunch. We decided to cross to Portland, so as to be in a good position to blast along Chesil Beach as soon as the weather allowed. The bay was incredibly busy with the horizon full of sails of all sizes and colours. It seems we had managed to time our crossing of the whole area just as the pre-Olympic trial races were going on. It was similar to running across a main motorway, whilst dragging a tyre! We were particularly concerned as the fast dinghies came through because they were accompanied by their coaches in RIBs. The coaches were mainly interested in looking sideways at their sailors, not ahead to where they were going.

We survived the fleets and then fought our way against a stiffening breeze into the lee of the old naval base for a welcome break. After that, we had a lively passage down the east coast of the Isle of Portland as far as Church Ope Cove, which promised a possible camp site amongst yet more beach huts. The landing was another wet experience; so much for all our dry kit! At the left end of the beach, some youths appeared to be trying to kick in a beach hut door, but they desisted as we landed and we thought no more of it as we set up camp at the back of the cove. Discovering a standpipe and a public toilet was a real bonus; no having to walk up the cliff path in search of water that night! Rain drove us into the tents, and I dozed off… to be awoken by the sound of 'Apocalypse Now' revisited. There were helicopters all over the sky and then we became aware of policemen and firefighters running up and down the beach (chasing and catching some local wildlife).

A little while later we were approached by a policeman (who turned out to also be ex-Army) and asked if we had seen anything. It seemed that after we had disappeared from view, the youths at the end of the cove had gone back to breaking into the beach hut and then set fire to it. This had been seen by some other youngsters, who called the police and then it all developed into what we had woken up to. Sadly, I could not help; it being before my eye cataract operation, I had seen the activity early on, but had no chance of identifying anyone. The rest of the evening and night passed quietly, if decidedly damply.

Saturday 11 June dawned fine and fair, so we set off to the tip of Portland Bill. I had my doubts about being able to go any further because the winds over the last few days were certain to have built up an unpleasant sea state west of the Bill, making a no-landing zone that could stretch to Bridport, nearly 20 miles further along. And so it turned out to be. As the final straw, the wind started to rise as we got to the tip, with some fierce sky streaks underlining what was coming in 'later'. Turning back was an easy decision to make. We landed as near as we could to the tip, and climbed up on to the grass shelf to see the view, get a weather forecast and have a think. Portland Race was in full flow, with the west-going tide kicking up against the incoming wind. The forecast we got was dispiriting; a deep depression was setting in, giving about five days of adverse winds. This in turn would kick up such a sea state west of Portland that we would probably have to wait a full week before being able to move on.

We set off back up the east side of Portland, thinking

hard. It actually was not too difficult; we only had 11 days left available to us, so losing even five or six would be desperate. In reality we had no hope whatever of reaching Ilfracombe this time around. Given that Barry 'does not do inactivity', I turned to him and said 'you'll go mad if we have to sit in Church Ope Cove for five days, won't you?' He agreed, so the decision to stop was an easy one for me to make, although I think Barry was surprised at how easily I made it. One factor which helped me was that after 2008 I was never going to circumnavigate Great Britain in the style to which I had aspired, so one more section here or there was of little emotional consequence. Stopping in the sunshine and rising wind behind the old naval base again, we both phoned our respective wives – Barry to give Wendy the news, and me to arrange for Carol to come and pick us up that afternoon.

And that is what happened; we landed at Castletown, in Portland Harbour, chatted with a number of divers and got sorted out in the sunshine, occasionally chasing kit across the car park as the wind took it. Everyone there agreed that the forecast was dire; the yachtsmen were talking of at least a Force 8 westerly coming through the following morning, with days of Force 6 and 7 thereafter. Carol arrived a few hours later, having established that we were no longer in Church Ope Cove, but rather now back in Portland Harbour and we retired in relatively good order to Carol's mother's house. As we moved, it was arranged that Barry would get a flight north from Bristol the following day, and Carol and I would bring the boats and kit north a little later.

And so 'The Last Quarter 2011' became 'the seventh

eighth'. We had paddled 287 miles in 20 paddling days of a 31 day expedition, giving us a paddling day's average of only 14 miles. This is quite low, but inevitable given the number of days we lost to the weather (something of a feature, it would seem, of this endeavour).

Another Tactical Pause

On the good side, Barry and I had proven to be compatible on expedition – something which is not a foregone conclusion when making extended trips with friends by any means. A couple of things were soon agreed. Firstly that we would pair up again for 'Round Three – the South West' in 2012, but with one important difference. Neither Barry nor Wendy found being separated easy and that wears away during a trip, giving both sides a less pleasant time than it should have been, either on the trip or at home. As a result, Wendy would be joining us in 2012. She is a competent paddler so that would not be a problem and she would, hopefully, raise the tone of the party. The second thing was that in 2008 Cath and I had eaten together in the evenings, giving me time and space to do the navigation. In 2011 Barry and I each 'self-catered', which I found left me with a lot to do in a short time. The solution was that we agreed that in 2012 we would cook together in the evenings. It seemed that my experience of curry would be likely to move to a whole new level!

Late in 2011, Barry and Wendy decided that they were going to rent a house in Ireland in mid-2012, so it would be ideal if the trip could be concluded in early June, weather permitting. And so the start date for 'Round Three – The South West' became late April 2012.

ROUND THREE

The South West

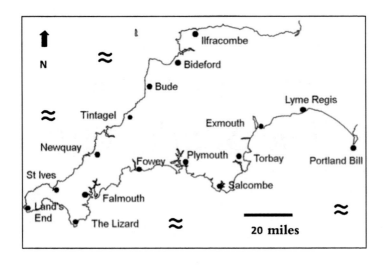

Map 12 – The South West

The South West

This whole section was going to be a new experience for me. Not solely in terms of the coastline, for I had paddled many small sections of it in the past, but also because I would be paddling with a married couple. I was described by one friend as 'the biggest gooseberry on the planet' – I do not think he envied my position of being the 'one' of a 'one and two' set up! Interpersonal relationships are what make, and potentially break, any expedition. If you have a strong relationship then no matter what happens you can get through it, with everyone supporting everyone else. Larger expeditions tend to fracture into small groups; whether these groups work supportively or in competition with each other seems not to be predictable. I have also discovered over the years that just because I am friends with two people, it does not always follow that they will be friends with each other. This was clearly not going to be the case with Barry and Wendy (unless something particularly dramatic happened!) but I was aware that although I had paddled with them individually and as a pair, I had never 'expeditioned' with them as a couple. Hopefully this would all be concern over nothing, but it was nevertheless at the back of my mind. John Dowd, a leading sea kayaker in his day, wrote in one of his books 'never take a friend on an expedition unless that friendship was born on an expedition'. He clearly had had a problem at some stage, although the details were never divulged in writing!

Notwithstanding all of those thoughts, we were all looking forward to the south west. By now I really wanted to get the circumnavigation done, Barry was looking forward to his reward for having put up with the scenically challenged section in the south east in the year before, and Wendy was excited about going on a long expedition. I had started to think of it all again in terms of a circumnavigation and, with several parties all due to attempt the trip in 2012, I wanted to make sure I finished as at most the 20th person to go around. A lower listing would be better, but there were several fast parties, including a couple of solo paddlers who were quite prepared to paddle in conditions far worse than I wanted to take on, going around in 2012. It was therefore not impossible that I would finish outside 'the top twenty'. Why this was important to me, I cannot explain. Perhaps the competitiveness from years of racing had not entirely gone away.

We planned to launch from the Weymouth area in late April but the weather had other ideas. Barry and Wendy had moved to Dorset, staying with friends until 'the off' and Carol and I were once again at her mother's house near Oxford. All of us were continually watching the forecasts and trying to pick a good time to start. The weather gods played with me yet again; a deep depression swept up the Channel in late April and then, most uncharacteristically, swung back on itself to loiter over the middle of the south coast. This took a few days to dissipate and tensions between us grew – we all wanted to get going. Although this year we all had open-ended diaries, Barry and Wendy did at some stage want to be in Ireland in the cottage they had rented, rather than spend the entire summer on a beach with me.

At last everything calmed down, so on the very last day of April we arrived on Portland and set up camp at the eastern end of Chesil Beach. The plan was to go to the tip of Portland in the morning, cross our track of 2011 and then turn west, heading for the last of my four corners. The sunny evening gave way to clouds coming ever lower and then the heavens opened. Because there was no wind, the rain fell heavily and vertically. We sought shelter under a spiral staircase to cook and eat dinner – with limited success!

The weather cleared during the night and we made good time down to the tip of Portland Bill along its west flank. After a few pictures we turned back and returned to the beach for a cup of tea and bacon butty then started on the trip proper. Chesil Beach is scenically challenged for 14 miles and although there was only a gentle swell running, it was sufficient to make any landing on the very steep shingle a dicey process. As a result we kept going until the bank rejoined the mainland and then, in the late afternoon heat, looked for a landing. Barry picked a spot and executed a very sporting landing, just managing to get ashore in good order but then having a dreadful time trying to wrestle his heavily laden boat up a steep bank and out of the reach of the swell. Once he had recovered, it was my turn. I was not quite so graceful. Although my timing was for once OK and Barry grabbed the bow of my boat, as I climbed out of the boat I stepped back and promptly went right under. I had found the edge of a ledge. Recovering, we fought the boat up the shingle and started to breathe more easily. Wendy landed gracefully and with style…

Our first real campsite was on the shingle but we had tremendous views stretching from Portland in the east to the hills of Dorset disappearing into the western sunset. It felt good to have started.

The following day dawned bright but with a stiff offshore wind. Launching precipitously down the shingle again, we stopped briefly after a few miles under the cliffs and then had a pleasant paddle under Golden Cap and across Lyme Bay to Lyme Regis. Sadly the end of the Cobb, a pier dating back to the early 1300's, did not on this occasion have Meryl Streep doing her 'French Lieutenant's Woman' act and we just had to imagine it. Lyme Bay is renowned for the fossils to be found on the shores and in its cliffs, so just after the town we combined a beach break with a fossil hunt. We found sections of ammonite pavement, some quite large, but the discovery of a plesiosaur was not to be ours. In the early 19th century, a local woman called Mary Anning made many important fossil finds and contributed greatly to knowledge of prehistory and evolution. The social mores of the day deprived her of the recognition she deserved and she has only lately been formally named by the Royal Society as 'the third most influential female scientist in British history'.

Within moments of leaving the beach we had slipped into another world – that of the Undercliff. This area, scene of many extensive landslips over the years, was atmospheric and tranquil. A truly beautiful and wonderful woodland wilderness.

Shortly afterwards we landed at the mouth of the River Axe and camped in Dorset for the last time on this trip. Here it was Barry's turn to get wet – Wendy's boat was taken sideways by a wave and he had to leap smartly out of its way to avoid serious leg injury. He jumped off the beach… Both of us were now looking forward to Wendy's dunking!

The section of Devon we traversed the following day was entirely damp, but we were rewarded with spectacular red cliffs sculpted into fantastical shapes by wind, sea and rain. The stacks of Ladram Bay made for a scenic backdrop for lunch and this whole stretch was an excellent reward for the shingle of Chesil. Having crossed the Exe estuary, I then had a major navigation 'off' moment. We landed a clear kilometre inside a bird reserve boundary and set up camp at the top of the beach. After a couple of hours we were approached by a warden who quite rightly pointed out, to my embarrassment, exactly where we were. He was keen that we move; we were less enthusiastic about doing so. In the end, after we promised that we would be gone at the crack of dawn, he decided that in true Nelsonian style 'I haven't seen you'. He was declared in my diary to be 'a splendid chap'!

We were still continuing with the 'red card' system of getting on and off the water if someone felt it necessary, and the following day it was mine that was played. I knew we had to move, but I felt really unwell, so we had only made a couple of miles to Dawlish when I knew I had to get off the water. Barry and Wendy were very understanding – I am led to believe I looked dreadful – so we landed at the back of a small cove under tall red sandstone cliffs. On walking into Dawlish, whilst I slept, the others discovered that we were camped in a private cove. Fortunately, this being west of the meridian, we were allowed to stay as long as we needed and the owners not only provided water but also charged our electrics. This was a complete contrast to some of the reception Barry and I had received the previous year and quite restored our faith in people. It was annoying to lose a day in the conditions – we could have reached Dartmouth – and to make matters worse a Force 8 gale was forecast for the following day. The wind only reached Force 6, but it was going in the wrong direction, so we sat out the day and finished it with a superb salmon meal courtesy of Team Bramley. I decided I quite liked the centralised cooking idea!

Many sections of the following day lived up to their reputations within the sea kayak community. Not only was the whole stretch down to Dartmouth wonderfully scenic, but the river running out through Teignmouth combined with the incoming swell to provide sporting conditions for a few minutes. A little further on we entered Torbay and discovered that the conditions, although benign elsewhere, were quite advanced both within the bay and at the headlands on each side. Leaving the south side of the bay was 'exciting' – we ran a wave train of breaking rollers around Berry Head itself and then discovered a long no-landing zone of wild seas beyond. Although enjoyable to an extent, the intensity of the conditions began to wear us down, both mentally and physically and it was with some relief that we were able to make an awkward landing on a horrible boulder beach just before Dartmouth. I had stopped looking at the scenery some time before, concentrating all my available energy on picking the line of least resistance through the waves and rocks. It was good to get on shore and feel the tension drain away. It was only then that we realised just how tired we were – finding somewhere to camp became a priority. Dartmouth itself is

Sheltering near Dartmouth. (W. Bramley)

Wendy takes off after lunch. (B. Bramley)

191

difficult for passing kayakers as there is just nowhere to pull ashore and set up a tent (or two). It seemed that there might be a small inlet just before the entrance to the estuary and that was where we found ourselves on a small patch of gravel only just big enough for two tents. Scruffy or not, it was home for the night.

A local inhabitant espied us as we set up camp and brought us, completely unbidden, a bottle of extremely nice wine. We rather hoped this standard of hospitality would continue. The weather was less welcoming and the following day, a Bank Holiday, was spent in the traditional manner – huddling from the wind and rain on a beach. Barry and Wendy walked to Dartmouth only to discover that it was, to all intents and purposes, shut. That seemed a little odd, given that it was the start of the holiday season.

One advantage with small beaches is that the carry to the water's edge is usually a short one – less than a boat's length in this case. We had a superb run south in sunshine with a breeze at our backs and going with the flow. The shingle beach of Slapton Sands passed quickly so we stopped at the bottom end at Torcross for a café coffee. After visiting the memorial to those lost in Operation Tiger, a 1943 live firing practice for the D-Day landings which became all too real when the assembled flotilla was discovered and attacked by German E-Boats, we had a fun run past Start Point and Prawle Point into the outskirts of Salcombe. We found a small beach at the mouth of the estuary and set up camp. The weather was deteriorating, as had been forecast, and we needed somewhere where we could sit out a couple of days.

Late that night my father died.

The death of a relative was one of those things that Cath and I had talked about before 2008. We both had elderly fathers and Carol's mother was of an age. The contingency plan for Cath in 2008 was straightforward – the expedition would stop and she would probably not rejoin me. Fortunately the plan was never tested for either of us. Matters were not any easier this time around as all three of us had elderly and ailing parents and Carol still had her mother. In some respects I had it the easiest of all as my father was in a nursing home very close to where he had been living with my brother Graham and sister-in-law Val. Finding out about my father's death by text was not the best way, but unfortunately the text message sent as a back-up arrived before anyone could call me once my phone was switched on in the morning. It was, however, not unexpected as dementia had been taking an increasing toll, to the extent that my father had not recognised either me or his granddaughter when we had last visited.

It was not a good day to be beached by a storm. Everyone was very supportive and Graham and Val were insistent that I carry on – there was nothing I could do to add to what was being done, and just sitting around was not an attractive option. Cath rang to offer any help she could give, including coming to my rescue if needed, but I reassured her that once we knew of the funeral arrangements Carol would be coming down and collecting me. It was good to feel her support. What we did need to sort out was somewhere for Barry and Wendy to stay whilst I went away and came back. A sandy beach was not the best option, but moving on from Salcombe would have to wait until the weather improved somewhat.

The following two days were wet and windy but enlivened

by two events. On the morning of the first day we went to a small café for coffee to discover that the other visitors taking shelter were not only from Yorkshire, but also from the very village that Wendy and Barry used to live in. As the conversation degenerated into 'ee ba gum' I fed the tame sparrows and robins pieces of the bun from my burger... Returning to the camp, by now wet through and somewhat sandy, I struck up conversation with a lady walking her dogs. When we reached the point where she asked 'are you the ones camping on the beach?', I feared it was about to go wrong. Then Sarah said 'it's a private beach and we don't normally allow it, but I've seen the writing on the kayaks and it's OK'. That was good and what followed was even better 'would you all like to come for dinner and a shower tonight?' Invitations like that are not refused, so in the evening we were treated to a wonderful dinner, preceded by a very welcome shower or, in Wendy's case, bath. Chris and Sarah Willis entertained us until late into the night and it was a real fight to drag ourselves outside into the wind for the walk back to our tents. Another case of people helping out just because we were there and very much appreciated.

At last we got out of Salcombe and paddled my favourite section of Devon coastline from Bolt Head to Bolt Tail. The cliffs here are continuous and the grey dappled rock was in stark contrast to the vivid yellows and oranges of the lichen in the early morning sunshine. Once we passed Bolt Tail and the little village of Hope Cove, I was on new territory as we headed along towards Plymouth. The shoreline dropped away flatter until we rounded the entrance to Plymouth Sound and ran in towards the city, helped by the wind that had swung from northerly to southerly as we rounded the corner. The Mountbatten Centre is an outdoor activity centre on the outskirts of Plymouth, and Cath now worked there having left her job with the Police. It was a wonderful reunion and she could not have been more helpful. Accommodation, drying rooms, catering and electricity all organised – what more could any expedition ask for? She had already done some shopping for me and now took Wendy and Barry to the nearest supermarket so that they could also restock. It had been four years since Cath and I had met, so we talked long into the evening before plain exhaustion overcame me.

I do not normally sleep well in buildings when I am on a kayak expedition; I seem to get very comfortable with the tent and then 'decompress' when I return home. This was an exception as I slept extraordinarily well and had more energy than for a long while. Cath saw us off from the beach, having agreed to come to the finish if at all possible, and then we turned to the west side of Plymouth Sound, making our way to Rame Head and Cornwall. We all enjoyed the colony of egrets on Drake's Island inside the harbour and then our progress became a little chilly as the wind rose and overpowered the sunshine. Just west of Rame Head is possibly the most beautiful cove in Cornwall. Accessible only by sea we threaded our way to the sand between pinnacles of rock, all the while watching fish and crabs beneath us. The water had a sparkling clarity and sun patterns chased our shadows over the seabed. It was a good place to have a break. The afternoon was less rewarding, consisting of a very long crossing to the outer edges of the Tregantle Ranges, closed on a Sunday, and then along a series of pocket beaches to Seaton.

This stretch clearly had attractions for gentlemen who liked to divest themselves of clothes… Seaton itself turned out to be a bit of a disappointment. There was nowhere other than the beach to camp and what was left of that at the top of the tide was not a pretty sight. There was no alternative, so we set to scraping two platforms in the grey gravel for the tents and started to think about what to do for Wendy and Barry whilst I was at my father's funeral, scheduled for a few days time.

Staying at Seaton was not an option, so the following day we battled against the wind for three interminable miles to Looe. I hoped to get help from people at the lifeboat station, but that was closed when we arrived. Then, by one of those magical coincidences, help arrived in the shape of a 'retained firefighter' who at that moment was scraping seaweed off the beach with his tractor. He and Barry struck up a conversation and within minutes Anthony was on the phone to his station commander and all of a sudden we had somewhere to stay for a few days – inside the restroom of the fire station! Even better was that the station was in the middle of town and accessible from a slipway just across the river. Not quite believing our luck we crossed the river and used the trolley to get the kayaks to our temporary home. Here things just got better – a painter working on the house next door said 'do you need somewhere to put the boats? My mate's got a garage just around the corner!' And so we set up camp in the fire station with our kit drying in the showers, ourselves clean and the kayaks safely under lock and key. It was quite an overwhelming experience – hats off to the firefighter network! In the evening we explored the town, finding the all-important pubs and pasty shops and discovering an art gallery – from which Wendy and

Barry bought me a picture of rough seas by a local artist as a memento of the trip. It was a really nice gesture and fortunately it could go into the car when Carol arrived.

Carol collected me the following day, Tuesday, and we were away at the funeral until she returned with me on the Friday morning.

Wendy and Barry had spent a pleasant few days getting to know Looe – Wendy had childhood memories of an earlier visit – and had also visited the mother of one of our friends further afield in Cornwall. The idyll of Looe was, however, shattered one night when the fire alarm went off and the crew turned out! Barry made himself useful by making a pot of tea for their return but no-one got much sleep that night.

Having retrieved our boats from the garage around the corner, we packed up and set off onto a not entirely good natured sea. Even had I not been away, we would not have paddled in the intervening three days anyway as a storm had come through and kept everyone, fishermen included, off the water. Later we were to hear on the news that had we delayed by just 24 hours, we would have been paddling in the harbour with a juvenile basking shark that decided to visit the town. We covered 10 miles that day passing Polperro and Fowey in the process. It was an uncomfortable paddle as the sea was extremely lumpy and Wendy in particular found it hard going. Reflected swell from the cliffs made for an unpredictable sea and also stopped us getting close in, so we plugged along about half a mile out, eyes firmly fixed on the headland marking the entrance to the estuary at Fowey. We mostly paddled reasonably close together but sometimes I found myself on autopilot and had to wait; after one such pause, Wendy asked 'how do you go so fast in this shit? – to which I replied along the lines that 'if I go fast, I spend less time in it!' I always had to bear in mind that I had much greater experience of paddling in advanced conditions than did either Barry or Wendy, and it would not be fair of me to expect them to cope with the extremes of what I could manage. That had been a particular topic of discussion before the start of the trip. I have had more than enough experience in big surf, both going out and coming in, in a loaded sea kayak, whereas they had almost none. It is not something that occurs often on the west coast of mainland Scotland, and when it does we try to avoid it! At the back of my mind was always the reality that their 'red line' was always going to be lower than mine. It was usually a factor which was left unsaid, but on one occasion near the end of the trip, I should have voiced my concerns much more forcibly.

Fowey proved, as I had suspected, a non-starter for camping kayakers, so we went round the next headland to what would have been a pleasant bay had not the storm brought in acres of dead seaweed. This was both smelly and unpleasant to land through and we and our boats were liberally sprinkled with small pieces of decaying seaweed. I would not have minded so much had not a gull decided to defecate on my, now rinsed, kit as it was drying. Sometimes Nature is just agin you!

On the following day, Barry and I were rewarded for our patience and earlier wettings – Wendy was well and truly trundled in the surf as we stopped for lunch, so much so that she did a complete change as she was wet through. Tact and diplomacy were the order of the day… Other than that the sea was much calmer than the day before, and the sun burst through in the late afternoon as we landed for a perfect camp on the turf at the back of Pendower Beach. Life took a turn for the better as the proprietor of the café gave us teas and ice-creams despite having just closed for the day. Our site was very reminiscent of the machair beaches closer to home, formed from the mixing of broken seashells with sand and fine earth. These make wonderful campsites but are a fragile ecosystem and easily damaged. Fires lit on such places will leave scars for a very long time and, sadly, there was ample evidence of that here.

Having been woken by the calls of northern divers, who seemed to be outside their normal range, we took advantage of a flat calm sea to make good progress down past Falmouth and the Helford River, ending the day just north of the little village of Cadgwith. It was a quiet day with not many vessels on the water, although some large ships were being unloaded in Falmouth with more at anchor in the roads outside. We also spent some time watching a combined RNLI and helicopter exercise – traditional activity for the rescue services on a Sunday. Our site at the end of the day left us perfectly positioned for rounding the Lizard should the weather permit. This was one of the cruxes of the trip, with a huge reputation for bad seas and sea kayak epics. In his account of the first circumnavigation of Britain and Ireland, 'Commitments and Open Crossings', Bill Taylor wrote at length of his party's misadventures here, including the only rescue that this group of highly experienced paddlers had to make during their entire expedition when one of their number was taken by a wave at the very tip of the peninsula. Cath had had her share of adventures here and for her it held the same position in her mind as Cape Wrath did in mine. This had stuck in my memory and I was quite wary of what we would find around the corner.

The aura of concern was dramatically lifted when Barry met a local, Martyn, also known as 'Nutty Noah'. This one-time fisherman turned artist and treasure hunter regaled us with tales of the sinking of his fishing boat and of finding a letter complete with a map of pirate treasure (we were camped above it, apparently). We tried to look suitably serious whilst he told us of the sinking and his subsequent rescue, but he was such a good story teller that before long we had aching sides from laughing and tears running down our cheeks. I suspect he has earned many beers with the telling of that tale in the pub!

Cadgwith was in a strange way another thread in my journey around the coast, for it was here that Monty Halls, he of Beachcomber Cottage fame, had made another of his TV series, this time looking at the fishing industry of Cornwall.

The Lizard, so fierce in my imagining, passed almost entirely uneventfully under a blue sky. We went 'with the flow' and had a perfect trip around early in the morning. What breeze there was came from the east, so as we reached the end, the turbulence of the sea dropped and we were sheltered from the breeze. It was easy to see where and why it could have been very different; across the end of the Lizard lies a submarine shelf, over which the tide flowed strongly with only minor ripples betraying the latent ferocity of the sea should a swell come in from the Atlantic. Our passage was uneventful, if quick, but it was nonetheless a relief to arrive on the west flank. Here the light picked out the wonderful colours of the

In Falmouth roads. (B. Bramley)

Martyn, aka 'Nutty Noah' - treasure hunter and raconteur. (B. Bramley)

lichen and gorse on the cliffs and cast deep shadows behind islets and towering stacks. There was no reason to hurry, so we threaded our way north amongst scenery tailor-made for sea kayakers' enjoyment to the small cove of Kynance. We landed to take advantage of the café for a mid-morning snack but I had overlooked that we were 'in the season' and prices had risen accordingly – we paid £20 for three teas and three baps! The rest of the day went well amid more stunning cliff scenery to Mullion and then Gunwalloe. Here the large pasty I had eaten at Mullion seemed to be taking its revenge – I had to get off, and stay off, the water. And so we camped at the end of a long beach, looking west into a leaden sun and almost within sight of the end of Cornwall.

The swell had gone the following morning, but so had the visibility so we navigated damply by ear along a featureless beach to Porthleven. Here we found a supermarket next to the slip in the harbour and restocked on food before heading west again 'to Mounts Bay and beyond'. We came across the first of the old mine works along this coast – abandoned chimneys and the tell-tale green streaks down the cliffs betrayed that it had once been a copper mine. These would become a feature of much of the coast from here on, relics of an industrial Cornwall which has all but gone. St Michael's Mount was visible off to our right as we crossed to Mousehole, but we were more interested in getting the crossing done as a stiff, cold headwind kicked up a wet chop into our faces. Our reward was tea and cakes in Mousehole before ending the day in Lamorna Cove where we found a patch of grass around the corner and out of the way. What I had not realised was that Lamorna Cove is privately owned. This became apparent during a conversation Wendy had in the evening with the chap who turned out to be the owner! He was pleasant enough about our being there, but I think he would have appreciated being asked first before we camped. He was rather more exercised by a TV production crew that turned up late in the evening to film an episode of an antiques show on the harbour car park – again without asking! His experience of people being there unannounced had not been entirely pleasant, with rubbish being dumped in large quantities and much damage being done. It is not surprising that efforts to pass a 'universal right of access' bill through Parliament meet some fierce opposition.

There was a long discussion that evening about our plans to tackle the next section of coast around to St Ives. Given the right tide and favourable weather it would be possible to do it in one long jump, but it was more likely that we would have to break our journey just after Land's End at Sennen Cove. The downside of this was that Sennen is world-renowned for its surf beach, potentially making a direct run to the beach adventurous in the extreme. Trying to avoid the worst of the surf by keeping to the south end and sneaking into the harbour is rarely straightforward, given a set of offshore rocks which regularly claim boats.

As it happened, we did not even get that far! After an excellent breakfast in the café we launched onto a lumpy sea and after one mile I was pleased to announce that I had passed the '2000 nautical miles around Britain' point, but celebrations were put on hold as the view unfolded. A heavy south westerly swell was breaking fiercely onto the cliffs and out to sea it was creating big green monsters as it passed over underwater shelves. That provoked some thinking, not all of it positive. We put in to Porthcurno Cove, keeping to the corner of the beach and even there being toyed with by the waves despite being assisted ashore by the RNLI lifeguard. After talking through what the swell would be like at Sennen, we re-launched and headed west. One mile later we turned back! The swell off the cliffs of Chair Ladder was enormous, with waves crashing up the cliff face and every cove was completely closed out by thunderous surf. I now actually became quite concerned about landing again in Porthcurno but all went well and we set up the tents in an alcove under the cliffs. It was warm and sunny but the swell was up and stayed up – as it did the following day, so we stayed then too.

Porthcurno is famous for two things. Firstly it was the terminus for the first submarine telegraph cables landed in 1870 as part of a chain which stretched from Britain to India and there is an exhibition in a building at the back of the beach showing the history of the telegraph. Secondly it is the site of the Mynack Theatre, renowned for open air performances of plays in an amphitheatre cut into the cliffs. It was built under the direction of Rowena Cade in 1932 for a production of 'The Tempest' and has continued in use ever since. On the evening of our second day, Barry and Wendy braved the cool wind and slight drizzle to watch the second half of a performance (they were sneaked in for free by one of the staff!)

Sleep that night mainly eluded me so I listened to much of the BBC World Service output whilst contemplating the next 'hop' to Sennen Cove. The wind was forecast to rise to a Force 6 north easterly 'later', meaning we should have most of the day before it came in and blew us way offshore.

Unfortunately the tides were now not quite so convenient in their timing and we would have to sneak along under the cliffs to the very tip of Land's End and then wait until they dropped and we could get around the last point and into Sennen. I was fearful that if the tides were slow in dropping and the wind came in early, we could be caught in a very exposed position, unable to go on or retreat. Never let it be said that circumnavigations are easy! I was very keen the following morning to get going early and make good time to Land's End; I had decided I was prepared to wait at the corner if need be, to make sure we got around at the earliest opportunity.

We got off early but there was concern that the wind was stronger than we expected (and wanted), so we flew along to Land's End without paying very much attention to the cliff scenery. I was not too worried about that as I had paddled this section many years ago, but Barry and Wendy would probably have liked to explore a little more. Our speed meant that we did indeed have to wait over an hour at the corner (right under a climb I had done 20 years earlier) until the fierce jet of water running through 'the gap' at the end dropped off enough to allow us to push through and around towards Sennen itself. In the interim I tried a couple of times to push through early and even tried a route through an arch under the cliffs but got ignominiously washed back on each occasion. As feared, the wind on the far side had increased so we had to push hard to regain the shelter of the cliffs before entering Sennen's harbour. Very glad to arrive, I threw myself on the mercy of some fishermen in the harbour (including, unknown to me at the time, the coxswain of the lifeboat). I explained what we were doing and asked if there was anywhere we could put up two tents for a short time. Soon afterwards we were set up in the pot yard – having done a spot of barrel and creel moving to make space! Terry George, the coxswain, made us very welcome and the offer of cleaning up in the crew room showers was accepted with alacrity. After that, there was little to do except eat, rest and work out the tides for two days time; we would be going nowhere in the Force 8 forecast for the following day.

Wendy and Barry went in search of a gas canister the following day, leaving me to read, look after the kit and eat ice creams – not a bad bargain, from my point of view. Their quest ended bizarrely, with Wendy being given a lift to the shop by a sheep farmer who had taken a shine to her... Late in the evening he turned up at the tents wanting to speak to her, so I retired to my bed and left the pair of them to sort that out! It was a good source of ribald comments for at least a week afterwards. Before that happened, the three of us met up for dinner in the local pub, where we discovered that in the whole of the village there were only five resident families. The remainder of the houses are seasonal lets, with one individual owning no fewer than 19 houses. It is little wonder that not only are coastal communities such as this dying out but that to all intents and purposes they are deserted ghost towns much of the year. This resonated very strongly with me, reminding me as it did of the deserted estate of Shellness on the Thames.

After a night's peace broken only by insomniac gulls and a lone lobster pot boat being launched at a very early hour, we enjoyed a pleasant breakfast in the sunshine waiting for the tide to turn in our favour. When it did, we sped across the bay to Cape Cornwall doing the three miles in 40 minutes, almost

Camping in the pot yard at Sennen Cove. (B. Bramley)

Resting after Tintagel Head. (B. Bramley)

without effort. From here onwards I was in unknown territory, having often climbed on the cliffs in this area but never having paddled here before. Cape Cornwall in combination with Land's End represented the last of my 'four corners', so from here on we were truly on the home straight. Barring any sting in the tail, it was all downhill and plain sailing from here to Ilfracombe.

We still had to get onto the true north coast and the section from Sennen to St Ives proved a delight. The cliffs were spectacular, the weather agreeable, the seals abundant and the tide in our favour. All in all it was a good run for 15 miles and we were very pleased to set up the tents under the cliffs on the outskirts of town. Here Wendy had a small mission to complete; one of the trials of camping by the sea is salt corrosion of tent poles and their subsequent failure – often spectacularly explosive. We had had a number of pole sections self-destruct along the way and Wendy had arranged to have some spare poles sent to us, to be collected from a pub in St Ives. This plan worked and it was a happy pair who returned to the tents bearing the new poles and clearly having celebrated their arrival!

Things started less well the following day, but ended nicely:

'Evil start crossing Carbis Bay in a Force 4/5 beam wind. Had to go right round the back and even then it was still very hard. Wendy struggling in the wind. Finally got some help from the wind and made good progress passing Portreath, then St Agnes and into Trevaunance. Very tired all round from the starting wind. Tremendous bit of coast – wonderful scenery, tiny little coves and lots of industrial archaeology. Arriving in

Trevaunance was bizarre – a simple request to Tony the lifeguard resulted in a place to camp (courtesy of Stuart Whitlock), free teas (Matt in the café), showers in the surf lifesaving club and more advice and weather forecasts than you could imagine. Everyone was falling over themselves to help. What a difference from the south east!'

In one of those coincidences difficult to believe, as we had pulled in to a small cove for lunch we were greeted by two people we had been meeting off and on for a week. Lynette and Andy, both police officers on holiday, were walking the south west coast path and we had now bumped into each other in Lamorna, Porthcurno and Sennen before this last encounter.

The next day was a long pull along the north coast; fortunately the world famous surf beaches of Perranporth and Fistral were benign. We were clearly having a good run of luck with the lack of surf. As the day wore on, we wore down and it was with some relief that we rounded Trevose Head and pulled into the beach of Mother Ivey's Bay. The name was first used in 1870 and reputedly refers to a local woman thought by many to be a white witch. This was another of those places considered a private beach, so it was perhaps fortunate that we were only noticed as we left the following morning. In the evening I changed over the chart I was using to navigate and went on to my very last one; according to several turns at measuring what was we left, we were 62 miles from the finish line. That distance ought not to take very long, and all our minds turned to the end of the trip and what lay beyond.

Daylight came and with it a fine mist thick enough to seriously impede our visibility but so thin that the glare of the sun caused us difficulty in the diffuse light. It became a morning of 'sunglasses on, sunglasses off' as we slowly made progress, passing the Padstow estuary with its Doom Bar before a pasty lunch in Port Isaac. The harbour was packed with tourists, much to the obvious irritation of the local fishermen, so we stayed only long enough for a quick break before getting away. Visibility in the afternoon was much better so it was a delight to paddle along the cliffs towards the huge headland of Tintagel. This is a serious point in anything other than a flat calm and even on this day there was latent feistiness lurking at every corner. Around the headland we found a small cove for a break; it was only when he landed that Barry discovered the patches of quicksand that lurked to greet him. Nevertheless it was good to stretch out for a while.

The entrance to Boscastle, our destination for the day, can be quite hard to find from seaward. Fiona Whitehead on her circumnavigation had looked in vain for some time in rough seas before giving up and paddling on to land through huge surf in Crackington Haven, four miles further north. Fortunately we had no such problems and entered the harbour easily. It was, however, mostly dry at that stage of the tide so there was a great deal of dragging over seaweed followed by some hard trolley work to get the boats ashore. After asking at the Witchcraft Museum, we were allowed to camp on the boat park – and given free cream teas in the café followed by use of the showers and washing machines in the youth hostel. Given the history of hardship and disaster in Boscastle, such generosity was outstanding. In August 2004 the village was hit by a flash flood resulting in widespread damage and 91 people being rescued, many by helicopter. Markers high on the walls of many of the buildings indicated the level the flood water reached. The village was again flooded in 2007, but to nowhere near the same extent.

With 46 miles left to go, we started the following day with hopes of taking that down a long way, initially getting a good push from the wind, tide and swell. Unfortunately we had to land in Crackington Haven to give Wendy's back a rest; it seemed that the labours of getting the boats back to the sea had been a bit too much for it. Rest and medications did the trick so we restarted and headed for Bude. Part way across the bay it became apparent that the swells were in fact large, if not sometimes huge. This was going to make landing unpleasant at best, so we diverted to the most sheltered part of the beach we could see and landed. Unwittingly we had all landed over an extensive area of rock shelves which would prevent us leaving at anything other than high tide, so we had to go back out and round into the sand of Widemouth Bay. This is a surf beach. I had a good long run in but both Barry and Wendy capsized, with Barry rolling successfully and Wendy swimming. Both were a little subdued after their first real introduction to Cornish surf. I was just glad it had taken so long to find us! In light of the rising wind and surf, and despite only having moved eight miles, we made camp at the top of a particularly scruffy beach and pondered our next move. There are limited options between here and Hartland Point 15 miles to the north; all the beaches attract surf, some more so than others.

Initially it seemed that we would not move the following day. The surf had dropped off a little but the visibility came and went and this was not a section of coastline I wanted to be on and not be able to see where I was going. I had absolutely no desire to repeat my experience north of Aberdeen where I was taken by big surf into an area I could not see, to land on a shore I could not see either. Breakfast in the local café was bought for us – yet more totally unprompted generosity – and then a visit to the lifeguard's hut brought a glimmer of hope 'I reckon this will burn off in an hour'. At least it started to, so we packed in anticipation of leaving. Looking at the map and taking the tides into consideration, it did not seem that we would make Hartland Point without having to take on its tricky landing in the dusk. Short of Hartland Point was a beach called Duckpool; we decided to make for there instead.

The Surf Guide to UK describes Duckpool beach as having good surf, as not being suitable for beginners and having fierce rips when a heavy swell is running. It would have been good to know that beforehand, rather than reading it when I bought the book after the trip was over. Had I known of its reputation, I would have gone nowhere near Duckpool. The three of us can however vouch for the accuracy of the guidebook's description.

We made good progress up the coast, taking in the scenery in the afternoon sun and managed to arrive at Duckpool at almost exactly the wrong moment. The swell running in was quite big and it was by no means clear where lay the best approach. Pausing to put on my helmet, I paddled across to a board surfer and asked for help. He directed me to another red-suited surfer, who turned out to be the lifeguard. After checking I really did want to go in, his advice was 'line up on the left hand flag, and get your timing right'. Having made

212

sure the others knew the directions, I left them putting on their helmets and started my run in. It was all a bit of an anti-climax; the surf did not seem too bad and although I had to wrestle the boat around a couple of times I had no difficulty making a reasonable landing. Hopping out of my boat, I turned seaward to witness aquatic carnage. Barry had let Wendy lead but had then been picked up by a wave and catapulted forward, almost alongside her. In his efforts to avoid a collision, he capsized. Fortunately he rolled back up and his time under water had slowed his boat down, allowing Wendy to pull ahead – whereupon she promptly capsized and exited her boat. As I made my way towards Wendy and her boat, Barry decided to show familial solidarity and capsized again, banging his head on the bottom but again rolling up. Determined not to be left out of the show, I got caught on the shoreward, wrong, side of Wendy's flooded boat and had to throw myself in the water to avoid injury. I rather suspect the surfers thought they had just seen the seaside edition of the Muppet Show, but they managed to hide most of their amusement!

We made our way to the lifeguard hut at the top of the beach and were made very welcome by Ollie the lifeguard and the rest of his crew. The little patch of flat stones by the hut was the only place we would be able to camp, and even then we would be only just above the high tide. The lifeguards did have some unwelcome news – the weather was deteriorating and a strong south easterly was forecast for the following day, with an increasing westerly swell. The two would inevitably interact in opposition and might well create 'interesting' conditions. (I have since decided that surfer 'interesting' most closely equates to sea kayaker 'terrifying'.) We were all thoughtful whilst sitting on the lifeguard's deck chairs contemplating the sunset that evening.

Potentially our second last on the water, the following day got high marks for planning, low marks for execution and went off the scale for adventure. The plan was to launch early in the morning, work up the coast to Hartland Point, arriving at slack water. We would then use the tide to push along to Clovelly, keeping close in under the cliffs to get shelter from the south easterly wind. Standing next to the boats at the water's edge, it became apparent that what had looked 'pretty big' from the top of the beach was, in fact, enormous. The surf coming in was not continuously big, but when the bigger sets came through, they were frightening. Good timing was clearly the key to getting off the beach safely. We agreed that I would lead, then Wendy and lastly Barry would follow. We would meet up at least 100 metres outside the break to make sure we did not get inadvertently picked up by a rogue swell breaking early. Any idea of a slow warm up went by the board as I lit the afterburners and went for it. Each line of surf was bigger than the one before and each needed a big pull on the paddles to get over. Just as I thought I had made it without too much difficulty, the last line of surf reared up over my head and I took an enormous wallop on my chest and head as I fought my way through it. Snorting seawater from my nostrils and trying to shake it from my ears I made it into the green water beyond and took stock. I had a problem. Somehow, in that last big hit, my spare paddle had come loose at the cockpit end and was now sticking out at 45 degrees to my left, out of reach. I really could not understand how the paddle had worked its way forward and it was hours later that I realised that it had not gone forward but rather that the deck bag to which this end had been strapped had been slammed back by the last hit, freeing the paddle. After much fruitless wiggling of the blade with my main paddle, I gave up trying to recover it – one of the others would have to help. Meanwhile, I saw Wendy coming out through the surf. She appeared over the top of about five lines of surf and then – nothing. Something had gone wrong, but I could not see what was happening as the building swells were now giving me cause for concern. Sitting far enough out to avoid the break, I was exposed to the wind and far from being south easterly, it was now blowing fully offshore. As each swell passed under me it would rise up, crest and then break with a thunderous roar. The tops of the break were swept up by the wind, creating a thin green veil through which the sun shone, casting transient rainbows over the surface around me. The very tops were whipped away in a white tracery curtain and it is to my immense regret that I never had the presence of mind to take a picture. It was a beautiful scene, but rather frightening.

For fully 45 minutes I sat there, eventually getting my spare paddle back under control by dint of a lot of wiggling, wondering all the while what was happening. Had I switched on my radio, I would have found out, as Barry made several attempts to contact me… Eventually I decided that I would have to go back in to find out what was happening; it really was the last thing I wanted to do. Timing was going to be even more critical as aerial combat in a loaded sea kayak in a big break is not an activity which often has a happy ending. I got away with it for almost the whole way in, but as the wave I was on hit the last sandbar, it reared up and toyed with me. I stayed upright but sideways inside the green tube and then everything went dark and wet. Upside down, forced back across my rear deck with only one hand on my paddle and occasionally hitting the bottom with my head, I decided to bail out. That was easier said than done, as my chart case and deck bag were now pinned over the spraydeck release tab. It is surprising how long you can make your arms if you really need them to be long! My only capsize of the entire trip, as it turned out. Spitting and snorting sand, in knee deep water, I followed my boat to shore and the reception party of Wendy, Barry and the lifeguards. I was wet, cross and sore. I was somewhat mollified to discover that Wendy too had had an unpleasant experience. Just as she and Barry thought she had made it, a huge wave rose up, broke and reverse pitchpoled her, sending her backwards end over end. She came out of her boat to see it going rapidly to shore whilst she and her paddle were in a rip current going rapidly to seaward. Had she not been spotted by a board surfer and rescued, she would have ended up out next door to me but without her boat…

Wendy had been badly shaken by the experience and her boat had suffered in the impacts it received; one of the hatches had imploded and was full of sand. This took some time to sort out, hence the delay. Ollie and his deputy came up with a cunning plan. He would in turn hold each of our bows steady in chest deep water whilst his deputy took his board outside the break and signalled when there was a lull in the sets. All we had to do then was paddle like hell and get offshore. The plan worked and fully one and three quarters of an hour after starting, we were all outside the break, 'shaken and stirred'!

This delay meant we would arrive at Hartland two hours after the slack, just as the maximum flow rate was starting, so there was no time to lose and we pushed very hard for the next few miles. Getting into the quay at Hartland was not straightforward as the swells were running in diagonally and exploding in one corner of the tiny beach. We hugged very close to the rocks on the other side to avoid the worst of it but Wendy in particular found it very stressful. The worsening weather meant we did not stay long and even so the disturbed water at Hartland Point itself was immense; we danced a fine line between the edge of the breakers and the fang-lined shore. As we had lunched, a lone paddler had landed and chatted to us. What he said gave us cause for concern 'me and my mate were going to Lundy, but it looked a bit too rough, so I came back'. This implied that somewhere out on the sea, attempting one of the major sea kayak crossings of the British Isles was a solo paddler, in deteriorating conditions. Fortunately, just before we rounded the point, a lone paddler came into view and we exchanged pleasantries as we passed. He was indeed the 'other half' of the equation; he had gone no more than a mile before realising that what he was doing was far from sensible, so he returned. Glad that he had come back safely, we rounded the point but instead of our expected relief from the conditions, we found a whole new set of problems. Far from being a south easterly wind, it had backed and was now fully easterly – straight into our faces. Even under the cliffs, avoiding the full Force 7 blowing in open water, it was a steady Force 5 and a real struggle to paddle into. Secondly, with the flood tide now at maximum flow, there was now a gigantic back eddy formed behind the point and that too was working against us. The next five or six miles were some of the hardest I have ever experienced; we worked close in, trying to keep out of the flow and wind but as a result having to avoid isolated rocks and reefs. These were hard to see in the conditions and it was impossible to relax. Nearly spent, we got ashore on a gravel beach washed by the larger swells and rested our heads for a little while. There was no option but to carry on to Clovelly, however, and these last two miles were almost too much for Wendy. Pulling ahead as I was getting too cold paddling slowly in these conditions, I landed in Clovelly and fortunately straightaway met the Harbour Master, Stephen. We could camp on the beach, have access to showers and a toilet, and there was a hotel doing bar meals for the evening, so no cooking would be required.

I pulled back out from the harbour, saw Wendy and Barry in the distance making slow but sure progress, and paddled to the beach where we would camp. I made a complete mess of the landing, getting soaked yet again, and was only able to get my flooded boat part way up the shingle. As I stood wearily up, Wendy and Barry arrived. I am notoriously slow at picking up signals but even to me it was instantly apparent that there was 'trouble at mill'! Wendy was looking murderous and Barry looked 'concerned'. Quickly helping Barry ashore, I asked him to empty my boat whilst I got Wendy ashore. She was exhausted and so cross she was almost incoherent; there had been a spot of marital discord on the water all stemming from the strains of the day. She had done exceptionally well and gone beyond any sensible personal limit, but it had taken its toll. We got the boats clear of the tide and then set about finding somewhere for the tents, eventually settling on a small scruffy patch of ground behind some bushes. The morale boosting showers were 'difficult' that evening as Clovelly was, unbeknownst to us, having a power cut; I washed in cold water in the sink and the others waited until later in the evening. At least the restoration of power shortly afterwards meant that the hotel kitchen could provide us with a meal and something to drink! My diary concludes for the day with one word, 'knackered'.

After such an exhausting day, I was fully expecting my heart condition to flare up (had it done so, I would richly have deserved it) but I actually had a really good night's sleep. We were all stiff and sore in the morning and the forecast was again poor, so we declared a day off to recover and explore the picture postcard village of Clovelly, with its steep streets and donkeys. All was looking good for the next day, Monday, so there was a real expectation of finishing in the afternoon.

At two o'clock in the morning, with no warning, the giant butterflies shook their wings in my chest – I was in trouble again. It did not settle down and by eight in the morning I was in Barnstaple hospital, getting discharged, after being shocked back in to rhythm, at eleven o'clock. It seemed that I would have to pay a visit to a hospital on nearly every section of this trip! Getting back to Clovelly was not straightforward as it was a Bank Holiday and most of the buses were not running. I managed to get to Bideford and Barry collected me from there in a car he had been lent. As we drove back to Clovelly we admired the flat sea and blue skies… Because I had been under a general anaesthetic, albeit only for a short time, I was barred from paddling that day and the next, which also turned out to be a 'flat calm, blue skies' day until the evening when yet another depression rolled in from the Atlantic.

The depression in the weather was matched by the mood of the party; we were stuck in Clovelly the whole week! At least the poor weather meant we could no longer see the far side of Barnstaple Bay and the last headlands of Baggy Point and Morte Point, but there is not much to do in Clovelly for a week and buying meals started to become expensive. The tent poles on both our tents decided at this point to have an unbelievable number of breaks and it became a tedious feature of life in Clovelly to drop a tent, extract a pole, bodge a repair and then re-pitch it. Three a day was not unusual! A moment of light relief came when we discovered a 'beer and cider' tasting session in the hotel. After my ration of one pint I wandered back to my tent and settled in for the night. Much later on, a very giggly Wendy was escorted back home – under the 'affluence of incohol' and supported by Barry. She had misread the strength labels on the cider and had got stuck into a very pleasant brew, completely unaware that it was the strongest on offer that night!

The enforced delay could have been very tedious but fortunately the lifeboat crew adopted us and two of them, Rachael and Richard, gave us the run of their house. This meant that we had somewhere to sit other than the tents and also gave us access to the internet and weather forecasts. Gradually the forecasts improved and on Friday evening it seemed as though Saturday was at least a possible day for moving.

At the back of my mind were two, related, concerns. The wind that had been blowing all week was bound to have kicked up a heavy and long-lasting ground swell which would be hitting us diagonally from our left rear as we crossed the 12

Packing at Clovelly on the last day.

miles of Barnstaple Bay. It would be an uncomfortable, corkscrew passage and not one with which I was sure Wendy could cope. Secondly, that swell had to go somewhere and would effectively wipe out every beach in the bay with big surf, giving us nowhere safe to run and hide if things went wrong.

The day started tensely; Barry was all for moving and could not understand why I had reservations. I thought that Wendy would have difficulty in the conditions once we had moved out from the shelter of the headland, but was reluctant to actually say so. In the end, late in the morning I said 'to hell with it, we're off'. All of a sudden we made our farewells and packed our boats, launching just after lunch. I had called Carol and Cath, so both were aiming to be in Ilfracombe that evening but interestingly I completely forgot to tell each about the other – so both got a surprise when they met on the pier!

It was indeed a wild ride across the bay. I had estimated it would take about three hours but as I had feared, Wendy found the going very awkward and we ended up taking over four hours in all. At one point she did say 'I was beginning to think we should never have left the beach' but at least we made steady progress. Off to the right, all the beaches were wiped out in surf big enough to be seen and heard from a long way out. All at once, as I was ahead on my own, a huge grey shape broke the surface right in front of me and then rolled back under. Very startled I kept looking around, but whatever it was, I never saw it again. I did not notice any dorsal fin, but I had the definite impression it was mammalian. By now very alert, we reached Baggy Point. The scene of many a climb in my past, I knew that there would be no shelter on the southern side nor the tip, but that it might be possible to find a small nook on the north side, and that was where, after nearly five stressful hours on the water, we had a break. We could see Morte Point in the distance. A reef there sticks out some way so we would have to be much closer, past the sands of Woolacombe, before we could decide whether to go through a gap in the reef, or around the tip.

This was yet another of those 'finger across the tap spout' points and the tide was running strongly. The tidal stream was hitting the reef and being forced left at high speed. Here it ran against the underlying swell running in, kicking up into wild chaotic heaps of water that towered over us. There was no gap in the reef so we had no option but to 'run the bumps'; this trip clearly was not going to give up without a fight!

Briefing Barry and Wendy to 'stick close and turn hard right after that rock – it will calm down a lot there' we entered the stream. In most other circumstances it would have been a hugely enjoyable run, but by now all I wanted to do was finish, and none of us needed to do a rescue at that stage of the trip. It was actually all over very quickly – accompanied by a few choice words of description from Wendy – and then we found ourselves on flat seas being taken at some speed along the final section of the coast towards Ilfracombe. The sun came out, we had a clear view of South Wales, last seen by me far too long ago, and it was a simple run in to the finish line. I heard Cath before I saw her – she was bouncing up and down on the pier, whooping with delight, and then I spotted Carol on the end of the breakwater, taking pictures and waving. I was rather pleased to read the sign 'Ilfracombe Harbour; maximum speed 4 knots'; that will do me fine, I thought.

We landed in the harbour, with rather less water about than Cath and I had started out in, to be met by Carol, Cath and her boyfriend Trevor and the curious glances of 'Joe Public' who clearly did not understand what all the celebrations were about. I recall a lot of photography and some wine – although that may have come later!

After 224 days on expedition and 2118 nautical miles, my paddle around Britain was over.

Reflections

What did it all mean? Even now, nearly a year after finishing, it is hard to answer that question. I am pleased I did it, albeit not quite in the style I had planned, and there was quiet satisfaction at being the 19th person around (so I did get inside the 'top twenty' after all!), the oldest so far at 58 and the first person to do it with a Greenland paddle. Is there the inner peace that I sought and expected? – certainly not just after I finished, largely because of the way I ended up having to do it in three sections. In the end it became a case of 'for goodness' sake, get it done!'; apart from any other consideration, getting to and from south west England from the west coast of Scotland every year is an expensive and time consuming process.

Looking back after a year, there is more peace and more satisfaction. I have presented the tale of the journey at two major sea kayaking symposiums and it was well received at both. Apparently 'the jury of my peers' is less inclined to look harshly at me than I am myself! I think Carol is pleased I have completed it, but we are now of course both living with the question Audrey Sutherland posed at the very start of this book 'when I succeed, what next?' Hopefully I will be easier to live with until something else becomes a focus. Carol has certainly put up with more than anyone should have to.

To quote from T S Eliot's 'Little Gidding':

We shall not cease from exploration
And the end of all our exploring
Will be to return to where we started
And know the place for the first time.

However there still remains, if only in my head, that unanswered question; I know I have paddled around Britain, but have I completed a *circumnavigation*?

The 'Thank You' List

There are many people who have helped in this endeavour over the years, and on any list I am bound to miss out someone – if it is you, I apologise! – but the following earned a mention in my diary as having been especially helpful.

2008

Lucy Hamilton of Pole Position, Oban – web support throughout the whole affair.

'Spike' at Abereiddi, who offered Cath and I breakfast.

Barbara at Horton, who charged our electrics and regaled me with tales of the Amazon.

Jane at Dale Sailing School – an absolute star.

Viv and Mike at Moelgrove – showers, a shop run and electricity.

David and Joanne Ashworth of Clevelys, who bought us food and charged our batteries.

Laura and Duncan of the Luce Bay Holiday Park – three free nights in a caravan!

Rena and Alex of Drummore – showers, washing and general hospitality.

Geoff and Ann Turner – overnight stay and a shopping run.

Doune Lodge – showers and battery charging.

Monty Halls and Reuben at Beachcomber Cottage, Sand – outstanding hosts!

Simon and Rachel at Culkein – showers and battery charging.

Kevin the lobster pot man and Rachel the Harbour Master at Kinlochbervie – for everything!

The crew of Coastguard helicopter CGMU for the banter and a lift to Raigmore Hospital.

Mike Wells – A & E doctor at Raigmore and a WEMSI course graduate!

Ken Nicol and the Pentland Firth Canoe Club.

Pentland Sailing Club – hope we left it tidy!

The Harbour Master and Coxswain of the Dunbar lifeboat – letting us camp on Lammer Island.

Tantallon Campsite – showers and laundry.

Craig and his mate (and his mate's mum!) at Newbiggin – for wine, food, bath and laundry.

Ian at Saltburn Leisure Centre for free use of the showers.

Katherine of Marsh Farm, Saltburn – for permission to camp on her front lawn.

The couple at Walcott who let us camp on their car park.

The campsite at California for frequent showers.

Southwold Sailing Club – showers and hospitality.

Aldeburgh Sailing Club – showers.

2011

Thorpe Bay Yacht Club – showers and electricity.

The caretaker of Shellness Estate – 'we look after people with boats here'.

Jake Monk at St Margaret's Bay – shopping trip and advice.

Mark of the Coastguard Pub in St Margaret's Bay for finding me a gas canister.

The Burts at East Preston for beers on the beach.

Gillian on Hayling Island for kidnapping our washing.

The Commandant and staff of Lulworth Ranges – for the tea, the lift to Lulworth and for not laughing too much!

Christine Miller of the fish shop in Lulworth Cove who adopted Barry and I.

2012

The Warden of the bird reserve at Dawlish Warren – for being Nelsonian!

Katy of the Venus Beach Café in East Portlemouth, opposite Salcombe, for hot water for a wash.

Sarah and Chris Willis of Mill Bay for permission to camp, showers and an outstanding dinner.

Anthony of Looe – the retained firefighter who got us into the station (and the Station Commander for agreeing!)

Jad – the painter in Looe who got us the use of a garage for the boats.

Roy Stevenson – the owner of Lamorna Cove, for camping and an early breakfast.

Sharon of Terra Nova, who went out of her way to resupply us with tent poles.

Terry George – coxswain of the Sennen lifeboat for a place to camp and use of the crew showers.

Tony at Trevaunance – lifeguard, Chairman of the Surf Lifesaving Club and Chairman of the Quay Fishermen's Association – contacts, showers and electricity.

Mark in the café at Trevaunance for free teas and an early opening for breakfast.

Stuart Whitlock in Trevaunance for permission to camp on his grass.

Mark at the Witchcraft Museum in Boscastle for finding us somewhere to camp.

Everyone at the Harbour Light Tea Garden in Boscastle – the magnificent cream teas were all the tastier for being free!

Linda of the youth hostel in Boscastle for showers, laundry, drying facilities and electricity.

Steve Haydon, ex-Army, in the Black Rock Café, Widemouth Bay who paid for our breakfasts.

Ollie and the other lifeguards at Duckpool – for obvious reasons!

Stephen, the Harbour Master at Clovelly, for help and support.

The A & E crew at Barnstaple for re-starting me, yet again.

And, from a personal perspective, Colin, Jim and Lester in 2008, Barry in 2011 and 2012 and Wendy in 2012 for their company and support on the water, without ever forgetting those who I can never truly repay – Cath and Carol.

To all of you – thank you.